7-11

Maths
Dictionary

Paul Broadbent

Published by Letts Educational
The Chiswick Centre
414 Chiswick High Road
London W4 5TF
Tel: 020 8996 3333
Fax: 020 8742 8390
E-mail: mail@lettsed.co.uk
Website: www.letts-education.com

Letts Educational is part of the Granada Learning Group.
Granada Learning is a division of Granada plc.

First published 2003

ISBN 184085 9369

British Library Cataloguing in Publication Data
A catalogue record for this book is available from the British Library.

This book was designed and produced for Letts Educational by
Ken Vail Graphic Design, Cambridge

Commissioned by Kate Newport
Project management by Phillipa Allum
Editing by Jean Rustean
Illustrations by Ken Vail Graphic Design, Cambridge
Cover photograph: Telegraph Colour Library (Sarah Jones)
Photography: Ohaus corporation; Paul Mulcahy
Production by PDQ
Printed and bound in Italy by Canale

How to use this dictionary

The Letts Maths Dictionary is aimed at Key Stage 2 Maths students, although other students will also benefit from its clear explanations and interesting detail. Text and layout have been designed to make the dictionary easy to use, including many features to help you understand as much about the words as about the mathematical ideas. This will make you more confident when you meet the words in your reading, and when you use them in your writing. These features are described in the examples below.

Entry word, or headword
The main form of the word. Unusual forms of the word are given in brackets after the headword.

Symbol
Any symbol or abbreviation of the headword is given in brackets.

Definition
The meaning of the word. This is kept as clear and concise as possible.

Topic area
The area in Maths in which the word is most commonly used (see full list on the next page).

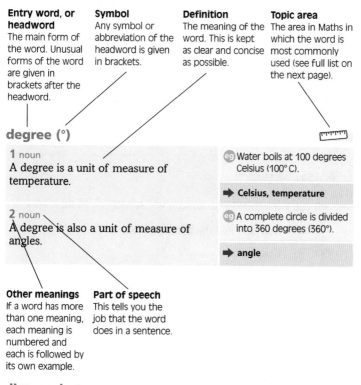

degree (°)

1 noun
A degree is a unit of measure of temperature.

eg Water boils at 100 degrees Celsius (100° C).

➡ **Celsius, temperature**

2 noun
A degree is also a unit of measure of angles.

eg A complete circle is divided into 360 degrees (360°).

➡ **angle**

Other meanings
If a word has more than one meaning, each meaning is numbered and each is followed by its own example.

Part of speech
This tells you the job that the word does in a sentence.

diamond ➡ rhombus ———— Cross reference entry
Go to another entry instead.

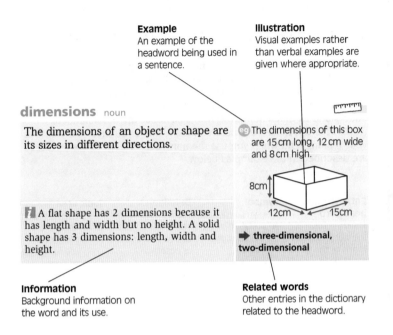

Example
An example of the headword being used in a sentence.

Illustration
Visual examples rather than verbal examples are given where appropriate.

dimensions noun

The dimensions of an object or shape are its sizes in different directions.

eg The dimensions of this box are 15 cm long, 12 cm wide and 8 cm high.

8cm

12cm   15cm

i A flat shape has 2 dimensions because it has length and width but no height. A solid shape has 3 dimensions: length, width and height.

➡ **three-dimensional, two-dimensional**

Information
Background information on the word and its use.

Related words
Other entries in the dictionary related to the headword.

Topic areas

Each entry is labelled with an icon which tells you its topic area:

1 2 3 4   Numbers and the number system

+√x⁻÷   Calculations

🗒   Shape, space and measures

📊   Handling data

? ? ? ?   Applying maths and general vocabulary

A

abacus (plural: abaci) noun

1 2 3 4

An abacus is a simple calculating tool. Stones, beads or rings are used to count and calculate. This example has beads that slide along rods.

ℹ In some countries abaci are still used to help calculate because they are quick to use. A **suan pan** is used in China and a **soroban** is used in Japan.

acute angle noun

An acute angle is smaller than a right-angle. It is an angle that is between 0° and 90°

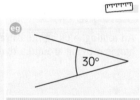

➡ angle, obtuse angle, reflex angle, right angle

addition (+) noun

$+\sqrt{x}-\div$

Addition is finding the total of two or more numbers. The + sign in a calculation shows that numbers are being added together.

The addition of 12 and 7 gives 19.
$12 + 7 = 19$

➡ sum, total

adjacent preposition

Adjacent means near or next to something.

For this set of number cards, 4 is adjacent to 9.

➡ beside

adjust verb

1 2 3 4

To adjust something means to change or alter it.

If you change the scale it will adjust the shape of a graph.

B C D E F G H I J K L M N O P Q R S T U V W X Y Z I

algebra noun

? ? ? ?

Algebra is a kind of language for mathematics that uses letters to stand for numbers. It is used to help solve problems and investigate number patterns.

If $y + 3 = 5$, what is the value of y?
$y = 2$

The multiplication sign is not used in algebra in case it is confused with the letter x. So 3 times n is written as $3n$.

➡ equation, formula

a.m. noun

The short way of writing 'ante meridiem' is a.m., which means before midday or noon.

The lessons started at 9:15 a.m.

➡ midday, p.m.

analogue clock noun

An analogue clock measures time using hands moving around a dial.

➡ digital clock

angle noun

The amount by which something turns is an angle. It is measured in degrees (°).

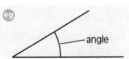

➡ acute angle, degree, obtuse angle, reflex angle, right angle

annual adjective

An annual event is one that happens once a year.

Your birthday is an annual event. It would be great if you could celebrate it more than once a year!

anticlockwise adjective, adverb

When something turns anticlockwise, it goes round in the opposite direction to the hands on a clock.

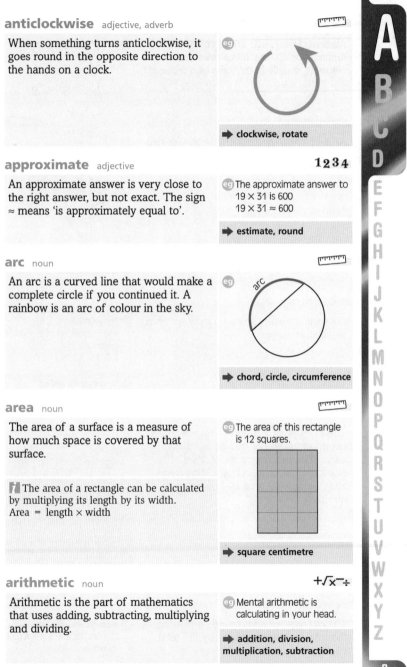

➡ **clockwise, rotate**

approximate adjective

1234

An approximate answer is very close to the right answer, but not exact. The sign ≈ means 'is approximately equal to'.

The approximate answer to 19 × 31 is 600
19 × 31 ≈ 600

➡ **estimate, round**

arc noun

An arc is a curved line that would make a complete circle if you continued it. A rainbow is an arc of colour in the sky.

arc

➡ **chord, circle, circumference**

area noun

The area of a surface is a measure of how much space is covered by that surface.

The area of this rectangle is 12 squares.

The area of a rectangle can be calculated by multiplying its length by its width.
Area = length × width

➡ **square centimetre**

arithmetic noun

+√x⁻÷

Arithmetic is the part of mathematics that uses adding, subtracting, multiplying and dividing.

Mental arithmetic is calculating in your head.

➡ **addition, division, multiplication, subtraction**

array noun

1 2 3 4

An array is a regular arrangement of numbers or objects. It has rows and columns, usually in the form of a rectangle.

eg
1	2	3
4	5	6
7	8	9

arrowhead noun

An arrowhead is a quadrilateral with two pairs of equal sides and an angle greater than 180°. It is sometimes called a dart.

➡ **quadrilateral**

ascending adjective

1 2 3 4

Ascending means going up in order from smallest to largest.

eg The numbers 3.2, 2.5, 2.3 and 5.2 written in ascending order are:
2.3, 2.5, 3.2, 5.2

➡ **descending, order**

average noun

The average of a group of numbers is a common (mode) or middle (median) value. The mean average of a set of numbers can be found by adding them and dividing the total by how many numbers there are.

eg This table shows the hours of sunshine for five days.

Mon	Tue	Wed	Thu	Fri
6	4	9	6	10

The mode is 6 hours. There are two days with 6 hours sunshine.

The median is 6 hours (4, 6, **6**, 9, 10).

The mean is 7 hours. $(6 + 4 + 9 + 6 + 10) \div 5 = 7$

➡ **mean, median, mode**

average speed noun

The average speed is found by dividing the total distance travelled by the total journey time.

eg A car travels 150 km in 2 hours. Its average speed is 75 km/h.

axis (plural: axes) noun

An axis is the horizontal or vertical line on a graph. The axes are used to measure the position of points on the graph. The x-axis is the horizontal axis and the y-axis is the vertical axis.

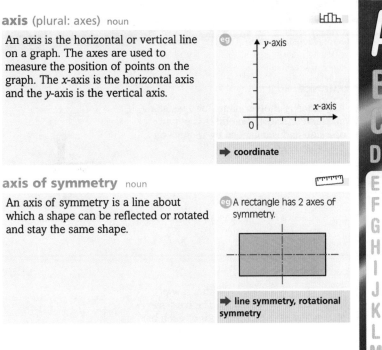

➡ coordinate

axis of symmetry noun

An axis of symmetry is a line about which a shape can be reflected or rotated and stay the same shape.

A rectangle has 2 axes of symmetry.

➡ line symmetry, rotational symmetry

A
B
C
D
E
F
G
H
I
J
K
L
M
N
O
P
Q
R
S
T
U
V
W
X
Y
Z

Bb

balance noun

A balance is another name for a weighing machine or scales. An object is put on one side and is balanced by weights on the other side.

bar chart noun

A bar chart is a diagram with a row of horizontal or vertical bars. The bars are of equal width and the length of each bar shows a certain amount.

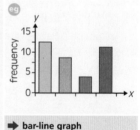

➡ **bar-line graph**

bargain noun

A bargain is a good deal when you buy something.

eg It was a bargain when you bought three books for the price of two.

bar-line graph noun

A bar-line graph is a bar chart where the bars are drawn as lines.

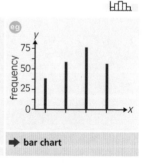

➡ **bar chart**

base   noun

The base of a shape or object is the bottom line or surface on which it rests.

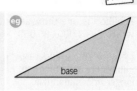

base

bearing   noun

A bearing gives the direction of a travelling object. It is the clockwise angle between the direction north and the direction being travelled. A bearing is always given as a 3-figure angle.

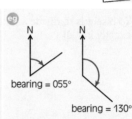

bearing = 055°

bearing = 130°

➡ **angle, clockwise**

beside   preposition

To be beside something is to be close to it or next to it.

The triangle is beside the square.

➡ **adjacent**

between   preposition

If something is between two other things it is in the space that separates them. A number between two others is bigger than the first and smaller than the other.

The number 45 is between 44 and 46.

beyond   preposition

To be beyond something is to be further than it or past it.

If you chose a number beyond 10000, it would need to be greater than 10000.

biased   adjective

A biased item is one in which all outcomes are not equally likely.

A 1–6 dice can be weighted so it is biased to roll on 6 more often than the other numbers.

billion noun 1 2 3 4

A billion is one thousand million. It is written as 1 000 000 000.

In the UK, a billion used to be a million million (1 000 000 000 000) but this is no longer in common use.

eg Saturn is just under 1.5 billion kilometres from the sun.

➡ **giga-, million**

bisect verb

To bisect is to divide a line, angle or area exactly in half.

eg This 60° angle is bisected into two angles of 30°.

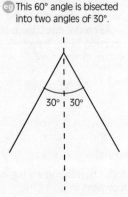

➡ **divide, half**

block graph noun

A block graph uses blocks to show the number of things in different groups.

eg

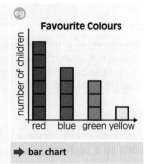

Favourite Colours

number of children

red   blue   green   yellow

➡ **bar chart**

bracket noun $+\sqrt{x} \div$

Brackets are symbols ( ) that put items or numbers together. In calculations, an operation within brackets is worked out before any others.

eg $4 \times (5 + 3) = 4 \times 8 = 32$
$4 \times 5 + 3 = 20 + 3 = 23$

➡ **calculate, operation**

breadth noun

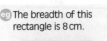

Breadth is another name for width. It is the distance across from one side to the other.

eg The breadth of this rectangle is 8 cm.

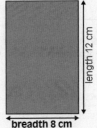

length 12 cm

breadth 8 cm

➡ **length, width**

British Summer Time noun

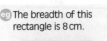

The period between March and October when clocks are put forward by 1 hour.

eg During British Summer Time clocks are changed to 7.00 a.m. when it is actually 6.00 a.m. for the rest of the year.

➡ **Greenwich Mean Time**

C

1 2 3 4

C is the symbol which stands for 100 in the Roman number system.

eg CX is 110.

➡ **Roman numerals**

calculate verb

$+\sqrt{x^-\div}$

To calculate is to use numbers to work out an answer.

eg Calculate the sum of the first five odd numbers.
$1 + 3 + 5 + 7 + 9 = 25$

ℹ The word calculate comes from the Latin word *calculus* meaning a pebble used as a counter.

calculator noun

$+\sqrt{x^-\div}$

A calculator is a pocket-sized computer, used for calculating.

eg

calendar noun

A calendar is a system for counting the years and dividing the years into months and days. Different calendars are used across the world.

ℹ The Gregorian calendar is used in most western countries. It counts years from the birth of Christ in the year AD 1, with 12 months in a year and each new year starting on 1st January.

eg

➡ **day, month, time, year**

cancel verb

To cancel is to simplify a fraction by dividing the numerator and denominator by the same number.

eg You can cancel, or simplify, $\frac{12}{15}$ by dividing both numerator and denominator by 3.
$\frac{12}{15} = \frac{4}{5}$

➡ **denominator, lowest terms, numerator, reduce, simplify**

capacity noun

Capacity is the amount of space in a container or the amount of liquid it can hold.

eg This jug has a capacity of 5 litres.

➡ **centilitre, gallon, litre, millilitre, pint, volume**

cardinal number noun

Cardinal numbers are the counting numbers. They are numbers that show quantity but not order.

eg The cardinal numbers are 1, 2, 3, 4 ...

➡ **ordinal number**

Carroll diagram noun

A Carroll diagram is a grid used to sort things into groups or sets.

🔺 A mathematician called Charles Dodgson invented Carroll diagrams as an alternative to Venn diagrams. He is better known as Lewis Carroll, the author of *Alice's Adventures in Wonderland*.

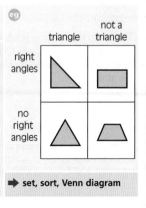

➡ **set, sort, Venn diagram**

Celsius – centilitre

Celsius (°C) adjective

The Celsius scale measures temperature in degrees Celsius, written as °C. It used to be known as the centigrade scale.

🔲 The Celsius scale was named after a Swedish astronomer, Anders Celsius. His first scale, developed in 1742, was the reverse of the modern scale; he used 100° C for the freezing point of water and 0° C for the boiling point.

eg On the Celsius scale, the freezing point of water is 0°C and the boiling point of water is 100°C.

➡ centigrade, Fahrenheit, temperature

census noun

A census is a count of a population.

eg A census is carried out in the UK every 10 years.

cent noun

A cent is a unit of money used in some countries. Its value is $\frac{1}{100}$ of the main currency unit.

eg There are 100 cents in one Euro.

centi- prefix

Centi- is a prefix meaning $\frac{1}{100}$. If it is written before a word it usually means divided into hundredths, or one-hundredth.

eg A centimetre is $\frac{1}{100}$ of 1 metre.

➡ milli-

centigrade adjective

The centigrade scale is used for measuring temperature. Centigrade is now usually replaced by Celsius as it uses the same scale.

eg On a hot day the temperature can reach 30° C, which is 30° centigrade or Celsius.

➡ Celsius, Fahrenheit

centilitre (cl) noun

A centilitre is a measure of capacity in the metric system. It is equal to $\frac{1}{100}$ litre.

eg There are 10 ml in 1 cl.

➡ litre, metric unit

centimetre (cm) noun

A centimetre is a measure of length in the metric system. It is equal to $\frac{1}{100}$ metre.

eg The width of your little finger is about 1 cm.

1cm

➡ **metre, metric system**

centre noun

The centre is the middle point of a shape or object. The centre of a circle is exactly the same distance from every place on its circumference.

eg

centre

➡ **circle, circumference**

centre of rotation noun

The centre of rotation is the point around which a shape can turn or rotate.

eg

centre of rotation

➡ **rotate, rotational symmetry**

century noun

A period of 100 years is called a century.

eg We are now in the 21st century.

➡ **millennium**

certain adjective

To be certain about something is to be absolutely sure that it will happen.

eg On a probability scale from 0 to 1, certain is 1.

➡ **probability, probability scale**

A B C D E F G H I J K L M N O P Q R S T U V W X Y Z

chance noun

The chance of something happening is how likely it is, or its probability.

eg There is a good chance that it will rain today.

ℹ If an event is impossible, there is no chance and the probability is 0. If an event is unlikely to happen it has a poor chance and the probability is between 0 and 0.5. If an event has an even chance then the probability is 0.5. If an event is likely to happen there is a good chance, with a probability between 0.5 and 1.

➡ even chance, likelihood, probability, probability scale

change noun

Change is the amount of money you are given back if you pay more than the price of an item.

eg This T-shirt costs £4.60. If I give £5 I will get 40p change.

chord noun

A chord is a straight line that joins the ends of an arc of a circle.

eg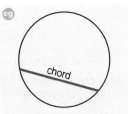
chord

➡ arc, circle, circumference, diameter

chronological adjective

When items are arranged in order of time, starting with the earliest, they are in chronological order.

eg These years are in chronological order:
1574, 1589, 1635, 1780, 1854

circle noun

A circle is a shape with every point at its edge at exactly the same distance from the centre.

eg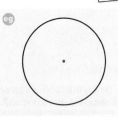

➡ centre, circumference, diameter, radius

circumference noun

The circumference is the edge of a curved shape, especially a circle.
The circumference is also the length of that edge.

circumference

➡ circle, diameter, perimeter, pi, radius

classify verb

To classify data or information is to arrange it into groups or classes.

To interpret data on traffic going past the school, we could classify it into types of vehicle.

➡ data

clear verb

The 'clear' key on a calculator clears the display ready for a new calculation.
If there is something in the memory this will still be stored until the calculator is switched off or the MC key pressed.

clear

climate noun

The climate of a place is the average weather conditions of that place.

The climate in Western Europe is wet and mild.

➡ temperature

clinometer noun

A clinometer is a hand-held instrument for measuring the angle of elevation (or depression) of something. It is used to work out the heights of objects such as trees and buildings.

clockwise adjective, adverb

When something turns clockwise, it goes round in the same direction as the hands on a clock.

➡ anticlockwise, rotate

column noun

1 2 3 4

A column is a vertical arrangement going up or down.

eg
```
1   2   3   4
5   6   7   8
9  10  11  12
```
The numbers in the first column are 1, 5 and 9.

➡ row

common factor noun

1 2 3 4

A common factor is a whole number that divides exactly into two or more other numbers.

eg The common factors of 12 and 18 are 2, 3 and 6.

➡ factor, highest common factor

common fraction noun

1 2 3 4

A common fraction (also known as a simple fraction or a vulgar fraction) is a fraction written in the form of two numbers, one above the other, separated by a line. The bottom number (denominator) cannot be a 1 or zero. It shows a division, with the upper number (numerator) to be divided by the denominator.

eg $\frac{3}{5}$, $\frac{7}{10}$ and $\frac{19}{50}$ are all common fractions.

➡ denominator, fraction, numerator

common multiple noun

1 2 3 4

If two or more numbers have some of the same multiples, they are known as common multiples.

eg Multiples of 3 include:
3, 6, 9, 12, 15, 18, 21, 24
Multiples of 4 include:
4, 8, 12, 16, 20, 24, 28
Common multiples of 3 and 4 include 12 and 24.

➡ multiple

compare verb

??? ?

When you compare two objects or numbers you look for differences and similarities between them.

When you compare a square and a rhombus, you see that they both have four equal sides, but the square has right angles.

compass noun

A compass is an instrument used to find the direction of north. It has a magnetic needle that always points to north. Once north is found, other directions can then be read on the compass.

➡ bearing

compasses noun

A set of compasses is an instrument used for drawing circles.

➡ circle

complement noun

$+\sqrt{x}-\div$

A number and its complement make a total.

To make a total of 100, the number 45 has a complement of 55.

➡ total

compound adjective

A compound figure is a mixture of more than one shape. To work out the area of compound shapes it is often easier to split them into rectangles.

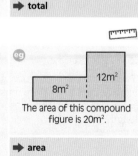

The area of this compound figure is 20m².

➡ area

A B **C** D E F G H I J K L M N O P Q R S T U V W X Y Z

computer noun

A computer is a machine for processing data.

ℹ The first mechanical computer was designed by Charles Babbage in 1835. The first electronic computer was built by Thomas Flowers and Alan Turing in 1943.

➡ data

concave adjective

A concave surface curves inwards, like the inside of a spoon.

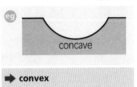

➡ convex

concentric adjective

Two or more curved shapes are concentric if they have the same centre point.

ℹ If you throw a stone into a pond it makes concentric ripples.

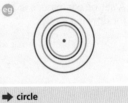

➡ circle

cone noun

A cone is a solid shape with a pointed top and a circular base.

➡ solid figure

congruent adjective

Two shapes are congruent if they are exactly the same. They must have the same size angles and sides of the same length.

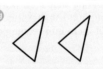

➡ similar figure

consecutive adjective

1234

Consecutive means one after the other in order.

eg 2, 4, 6, 8, 10 ... are consecutive even numbers.

constant noun

$+\sqrt{x} - \div$

A constant is a value that is unchanged when it is used.

eg 10x × (n) = = is a constant that can be set on a calculator to multiply any number (n) by 10.

continuous data noun

Continuous data is data arranged in groups with no gaps. It is often shown using a line graph.

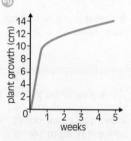

➡ **data, discrete data, line graph**

convert verb

1234

To convert something is to change it from one form to another. A conversion chart or graph can help work out the conversion.

eg To convert centimetres to inches, multiply by 0.3937.
1 cm = 0.3937 inches

➡ **exchange rate**

convex adjective

A convex surface curves outwards, like the outside of a spoon.

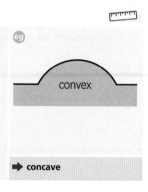

convex

➡ **concave**

A
B
C
D
E
F
G
H
I
J
K
L
M
N
O
P
Q
R
S
T
U
V
W
X
Y
Z

coordinate noun

Coordinates are numbers that give the position of a point on a graph or grid. The numbers are usually written as a pair. The first coordinate gives the distance along the horizontal axis; the second coordinate gives the distance along the vertical axis.

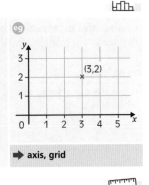

eg

➡ **axis, grid**

corner noun

A corner is a point where two or more lines meet.

eg A square has four corners.

➡ **vertex**

count verb

1 2 3 4

When you count you say (in your head or aloud) numbers in a certain order. When you count objects you find out how many there are by matching each object with a number name.

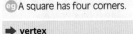

eg

There are 1, 2, 3, 4, 5, **6** spots.

cross-section noun

A cross-section of a solid shape is a slice through it at right-angles to one of its dimensions, such as its length or its height.

eg The cross-section of this cylinder is a circle.

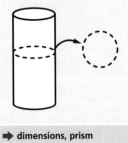

➡ **dimensions, prism**

cube

1 noun

A cube is a solid shape with six square faces.

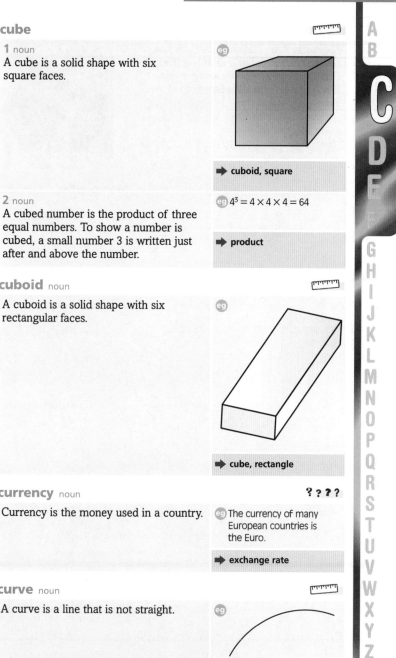

➡ **cuboid, square**

2 noun

A cubed number is the product of three equal numbers. To show a number is cubed, a small number 3 is written just after and above the number.

eg $4^3 = 4 \times 4 \times 4 = 64$

➡ **product**

cuboid noun

A cuboid is a solid shape with six rectangular faces.

➡ **cube, rectangle**

currency noun

Currency is the money used in a country.

eg The currency of many European countries is the Euro.

➡ **exchange rate**

curve noun

A curve is a line that is not straight.

cylinder noun

A cylinder is a solid shape with the same sized circles at either end. It has the same circular cross-section all along its length. If a shape is cylindrical it is shaped like a cylinder.

➡ **cross-section**

Dd

A B C **D** E F G H I J K L M N O P Q R S T U V W X Y Z

D
1 2 3 4

D is the symbol which stands for 500 in the Roman number system.

eg D + D = M

➡ **Roman numerals**

daily adjective

Something done daily is done on every day of the week.

eg Many newspapers are produced daily.

➡ **day**

dart ➡ arrowhead

data noun

Data is a set of numbers or information that can be collected, measured or recorded.

eg Lists of names and addresses are examples of data.

database noun

A database is a large amount of information stored in an organised way, often on a computer.

eg A database can be set up to store names and addresses.

➡ **computer**

day noun

A day lasts for 24 hours, starting at midnight.

eg There are seven days in a week.

24 hours is the length of time that the Earth takes to make one complete turn on its axis. The sun rises and sets once during a day.

➡ **daily**

dear adjective
? ? ? ?

If something costs a lot of money it is said to be dear.

eg The trainers were too dear at £78.

➡ **expensive**

23

deca- prefix

1 2 3 4

Deca- is a prefix meaning 10.

eg A decagon is a shape with 10 sides.

decade noun

A decade is a time period of ten years.

eg The 1990s was the decade from 1st January 1990 to 31st December 1999.

➡ century

decagon noun

A decagon is a 10-sided polygon.

eg

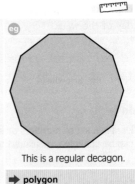

This is a regular decagon.

➡ polygon

decahedron noun

A decahedron is a solid shape with 10 faces.

eg

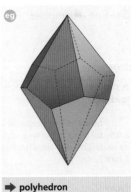

➡ polyhedron

decimal fraction noun

1 2 3 4

The part of a decimal number to the right of the decimal point is called the decimal fraction. It is a number less than 1.

eg 0.85 is $\frac{8}{10} + \frac{5}{100} = \frac{85}{100}$

decimal number noun

1234

A decimal number is any number made up of the digits 0 to 9.

eg 127.6 is $100 + 20 + 7 + \frac{6}{10}$

decimal place noun

1234

The position of a digit after the decimal point is known as its decimal place.

eg 1.845 has 3 decimal places.

decimal point noun

1234

A decimal point is used to show which digits are whole numbers and which are fractions. The digits to the left of the decimal point give the number of ones, tens, hundreds and thousands. The digits to the right of the decimal point give the number of tenths, hundredths, thousandths and so on.

eg 1632.951

In this number 1, 6, 3 and 2 are whole numbers and 9, 5 and 1 are fractions.

! Decimal points vary around the world. In France, for example, a comma is used instead of a decimal point.

➡ **fraction**

decrease verb

+√x⁻÷

If you decrease something you make it less or reduce it.

eg If you decrease a number by 20 you take 20 away from it.

➡ **increase**

define verb

You define something by explaining it, giving its precise meaning.

eg You define a quadrilateral by describing its properties.

degree (°)

1 noun
A degree is a unit of measure of temperature.

eg Water boils at 100 degrees Celsius (100° C).

➡ **Celsius, temperature**

2 noun
A degree is also a unit of measure of angles.

eg A complete circle is divided into 360 degrees (360°).

➡ **angle**

A B C **D** E F G H I J K L M N O P Q R S T U V W X Y Z

denominator noun

The denominator is the number below the line in a fraction. It shows how many parts a whole shape or number of items is divided into.

In the fraction $\frac{1}{4}$, the denominator is 4.
$\frac{1}{4}$ of 12 is $12 \div 4 = 3$

➡ **fraction, numerator**

depth noun

When something is at a certain depth, it is that distance under the ground or sea level.

The shipwreck was found at a depth of 40 metres.

descending adjective

Descending means going down in order from largest to smallest.

The numbers 47, 58, 39 and 61 written in descending order are:
61, 58, 47, 39

➡ **ascending, order**

diagonal noun

A diagonal line joins together two corners inside a shape such as a rectangle. The corners joined by a diagonal are not adjacent to each other.

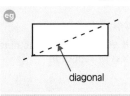

diagonal

➡ **adjacent**

diameter noun

The diameter is a line that passes from one side of a circle or sphere through the centre to the other side. The diameter cuts a circle in half.

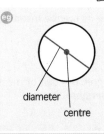

diameter

centre

➡ **circle, radius, semicircle, sphere**

diamond ➡ rhombus

die (plural: dice) noun

? ? ? ?

A die is usually a cube, with a number from 1 to 6 marked on each face. On a 1–6 die the numbers on opposite faces always add up to seven.

➡ probability

difference noun

+√x⁻÷

The difference is the amount by which one number or value is greater than another. You can also work out the difference between two numbers by subtracting the smaller one from the greater one.

The difference between 17 and 25 is 8.
$$25 - 17 = 8$$

➡ subtraction

digit noun

1234

A digit is any of the ten numerals: 0, 1, 2, 3, 4, 5, 6, 7, 8 or 9. Numbers are made up of digits.

The number 847 has three digits.

➡ numeral

digital clock noun

A digital clock shows the time using digits rather than by having hands on a dial.

➡ analogue clock

dimensions noun

The dimensions of an object or shape are its sizes in different directions.

The dimensions of this box are 15 cm long, 12 cm wide and 8 cm high.

A flat shape has 2 dimensions because it has length and width but no height. A solid shape has 3 dimensions: length, width and height.

➡ three-dimensional, two-dimensional

disc noun

A disc is a flat circular shape.

discount noun

$+\sqrt{x^-} \div$

A discount is an amount subtracted from the original price of an item.

The £48 coat has a discount of 50%, so it now costs £24.

discrete data noun

Separate or distinct groups or items of data are known as discrete data.

Shoe sizes are discrete data.

➡ **continuous data, data**

distance noun

Distance is the length between two points.

The distance between the two villages is 17 km.

➡ **length**

distribution noun

A distribution is a collection of measurements or data.

This chart shows the distribution of shoe sizes for a group of people:

shoe size	2	3	4	5	6
number of people	8	11	17	14	9

divide verb

$+\sqrt{x^-} \div$

To divide means to carry out the operation of division; sharing or grouping a quantity into a number of equal parts.

When you divide 15 by 3 the answer is 5.

➡ **division**

divisible adjective

$+\sqrt{x^-} \div$

If one number can be divided exactly by another number then it is divisible by the this number.

42, 81 and 105 are all divisible by 3.

division (÷) noun

Division is an operation on numbers in which a number is shared equally into a number of parts. The answer is called the quotient.

eg Division is the opposite of multiplication.

➡ divide, quotient

divisor noun

A divisor is a number that another number is divided by.

eg For 27 ÷ 3, the divisor is 3.

dodecagon noun

A dodecagon is a 12-sided polygon.

eg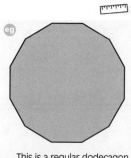

This is a regular dodecagon.

➡ polygon

dodecahedron noun

A dodecahedron is a 12-faced solid shape. The faces of a regular dodecahedron are regular pentagons.

eg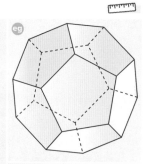

➡ polyhedron

double

1 verb
To double is to multiply by 2.

eg If you double 15 the answer is 30.

2 adjective
The number that is twice another number is a double.

eg The double of 4 is 8.

doubt noun

If something is in doubt, it is uncertain to happen.

eg When an event is in doubt it is nearer 0 than 1 on the probability scale.

➡ **probability scale, uncertain**

dozen noun

A dozen is a group of 12.

eg This box holds one dozen eggs.

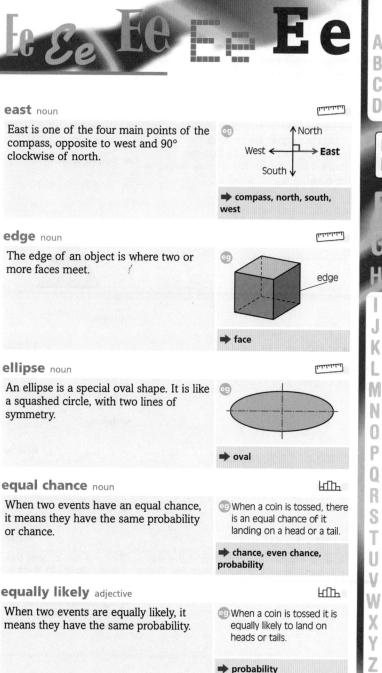

E e

east noun

East is one of the four main points of the compass, opposite to west and 90° clockwise of north.

eg

North
West ←→ **East**
South

➡ **compass, north, south, west**

edge noun

The edge of an object is where two or more faces meet.

eg

edge

➡ **face**

ellipse noun

An ellipse is a special oval shape. It is like a squashed circle, with two lines of symmetry.

eg

➡ **oval**

equal chance noun

When two events have an equal chance, it means they have the same probability or chance.

eg When a coin is tossed, there is an equal chance of it landing on a head or a tail.

➡ **chance, even chance, probability**

equally likely adjective

When two events are equally likely, it means they have the same probability.

eg When a coin is tossed it is equally likely to land on heads or tails.

➡ **probability**

equals (=) verb

+√x⁻÷

If one amount equals another they are the same.

eg 150 pence equals £1.50.

equation noun

+√x⁻÷

An equation is a statement showing that things are equal. Every equation has an equals sign which shows that the numbers on either side of it are the same or equal.

eg $y = 8 - 2$
In this equation, $y = 6$.

➡ algebra, formula

equilateral triangle noun

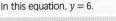

All three sides of an equilateral triangle are the same length. Each of the angles are also equal, at 60°.

eg

➡ triangle

equivalent fraction noun

1 2 3 4

An equivalent fraction is a fraction with the same value as another.

eg These are all equivalent fractions:
$\frac{1}{2} = \frac{2}{4} = \frac{3}{6} = \frac{4}{8}$

➡ fraction

estimate verb

+√x⁻÷

To estimate a number means to decide roughly how big that number is.

eg I estimate that there are 200 words on this page.

➡ approximate

even chance noun

If an event has an even chance, there is the same chance of it happening as not happening. The probability is 0.5.

eg When a coin is tossed, there is an even chance that it will show tails.

➡ chance, equal chance, fifty-fifty, probability

even number noun

1234

An even number can be divided by 2 without leaving a remainder.

All even numbers end with the digits 0, 2, 4, 6 or 8. So 1356 is an even number.

➡ **odd number**

exact adjective

$+\sqrt{x}-\div$

An exact number is the true value, not an approximate answer.

The exact answer to 38×17 is 646.

➡ **approximate**

exchange rate noun

? ? ? ?

The exchange rate is the rate at which the currency of one country is exchanged for that of another.

The exchange rate for £ (pounds sterling) to $ (US dollars) is approximately £1 = $1.60.

➡ **convert, currency**

expensive adjective

? ? ? ?

If something costs a lot of money it is said to be expensive.

The computer was very expensive to buy.

➡ **dear**

A B C D E F G H I J K L M N O P Q R S T U V W X Y Z

Ff

face noun

The flat surface or side of a solid shape is called a face.

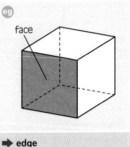

eg face

➡ edge

factor noun

1 2 3 4

A factor is a whole number that divides exactly into another number without leaving a remainder.

eg 4 is a factor of 12 as it divides exactly into 12.
12 has six factors: 1, 2, 3, 4, 6 and 12.

factorise verb

1 2 3 4

To factorise is to break up or separate a number into its factors. This can be useful for mental calculations.

eg 24 may be factorised into:
$2 \times 3 \times 4$ or
4×6 or
3×8.

Fahrenheit (°F) adjective

Fahrenheit refers to the Fahrenheit scale used for measuring temperature.

🔢 This temperature scale is named after G.D Fahrenheit, a German physicist from the beginning of the 18th Century. The boiling point of water on the Fahrenheit scale is 212° F and the freezing point is 32° F.

eg On a warm day the temperature can reach 70° F.

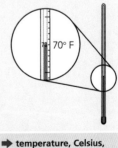

70° F

➡ temperature, Celsius, centigrade

fair adjective

When the outcomes of an event or item are equally likely, it means that it is fair.

When a coin is tossed it is equally likely to land on heads or tails; it is fair.

➡ **unfair**

Fibonacci sequence noun

1 2 3 4

A Fibonacci sequence is one where each number is found by adding the two previous numbers. The first two numbers are 1, 1 …

1, 1, 2, 3, 5, 8, 13, 21 … is a Fibonacci sequence.

Leonardo Fibonacci was a 13th Century Italian mathematician.

➡ **sequence**

fifty-fifty adjective, adverb

When there is an even chance of an event happening or not happening, it has a fifty-fifty chance.

When a coin is tossed, there is a fifty-fifty chance that it will show heads.

➡ **even chance, probability**

first (1st) adjective

1 2 3 4

The first is the earliest in an order.

The first even number is 2.

flow chart noun

A flow chart is a diagram that shows the steps you must follow to solve a problem.

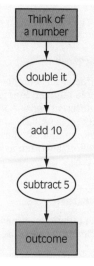

Think of a number

↓

double it

↓

add 10

↓

subtract 5

↓

outcome

foot (ft) noun

A foot is an imperial unit of length equal to 12 inches.

eg Most doors are just over 6 foot in height, which is approximately 2 metres.

A foot was originally based on the length of a person's foot. This was an easy way to measure a length of wood, but obviously the lengths varied with the size of the foot.
The Ancient Greeks and the Romans were the first to use standard units. The Romans made copper bars one foot long and divided into twelve equal parts as a standard unit, which probably matched the length of an emperor's foot. The feet and inches used in modern times are based on the Roman foot.

➡ **imperial system, inch, metre, yard**

formula (plural: formulae) noun

A formula is a rule that tells you how to work out something when you are given certain values.

eg The formula for finding the area of a rectangle is
area = length × breadth
or $a = l \times b$.

➡ **algebra, equation**

fortnight noun

A fortnight is two weeks or 14 days.

eg The home matches of my football team are every fortnight.

The word fortnight comes from two words, fourteen and night, joined together.

➡ **day, week**

fraction noun

A fraction is a number that is part of a whole number. Fractions can be written in different ways. A vulgar or common fraction is written with a numerator and denominator, such as $\frac{3}{4}$, and a decimal fraction is written as a decimal, such as 0.75.

eg $\frac{2}{3}$, $1\frac{1}{4}$, $3\frac{1}{5}$ and 3.25 are all fractions.

➡ **decimal fraction, improper fraction, mixed number, proper fraction**

frequency noun

The number of times that something happens is called the frequency.

eg The frequency of trains stopping at the station is three every hour.

frequency table noun

A frequency table or chart is a way of recording information. It shows the number of times something happens.

Car colours	Frequency
red	50
white	36
blue	53

This shows the number of different colour cars passing the school in one hour.

function noun

A function is a rule for changing one set of numbers into another. A function machine can be drawn to show functions.

The function for this change is × 2 + 1:

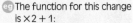
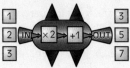

➡ **relationship**

Gg

gallon noun

A gallon is an imperial unit of capacity. It measures the amount, or volume, of liquids. There are 8 pints in 1 gallon.

eg A bucket holds approximately two gallons.

➡ imperial system, pint

geometry noun

Geometry is the part of mathematics that studies shapes, lines and angles. Geometrical shapes are made from straight lines and parts of circles.

eg A geometry set includes a ruler, set-square, compasses and protractor for drawing shapes.

giga- prefix

Giga- is a prefix meaning 1 000 000 000, or 1 billion.

eg A computer can have 1 Gigabyte of memory.

➡ billion

gram (g) noun

A gram is a unit of mass or weight in the metric system. It is a very small mass – there are 1000 grams in 1 kilogram.

eg A paper clip has a mass of about 1 g.

➡ kilogram

graph noun

A graph is a diagram that shows how one thing relates to another. Graphs often have a horizontal axis and a vertical axis. Graph paper has ruled square lines to help draw graphs.

eg

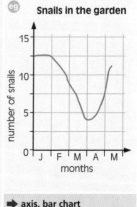

Snails in the garden

➡ axis, bar chart

greater than (>) phrase

1 2 3 4

If one quantity is larger than another, the first is greater than the second.

$\frac{2}{3} > \frac{1}{2}$ This shows that $\frac{2}{3}$ is greater than $\frac{1}{2}$.

➡ **less than**

Greenwich Mean Time noun

This is the local time for places on the same line as the Meridian of Greenwich, London.

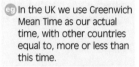 In the UK we use Greenwich Mean Time as our actual time, with other countries equal to, more or less than this time.

➡ **British Summer Time**

grid noun

A grid on a map or plan is a set of numbered or lettered squares. It helps find exact places by using coordinates.

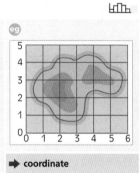

➡ **coordinate**

half (plural: halves) noun

1 2 3 4

A half is a fraction written as $\frac{1}{2}$. When something is divided into two equal parts, each part is one half.

eg $\frac{1}{2}$ of 16 is 8.

➡ fraction

halve verb

1 2 3 4

To halve something is to divide it into two equal parts.

eg If you halve a rectangle you can form two right-angled triangles.

➡ divide

hectare noun

A hectare is a metric measure of area. 1 hectare = 10 000 square metres.

eg A square with sides of 100 metres covers an area of 1 hectare.

➡ area

height noun

The height of something is how tall it is.

eg The height of a door is about 2 metres.

hemisphere noun

A hemisphere is half a sphere, made by cutting through the centre of a sphere.

eg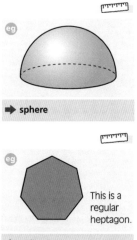

➡ sphere

heptagon noun

A heptagon is a flat shape with seven straight sides.

eg This is a regular heptagon.

➡ polygon

hexagon noun

A hexagon is a flat shape with six straight sides.

eg This is a regular hexagon.

➡ polygon

highest common factor noun

12**3**4

The highest common factor is the greatest whole number that divides exactly into two or more other numbers.

eg The common factors of 16 and 24 are 2, 4 and 8, so the highest common factor is 8.

➡ common factor, factor

horizontal

1 noun
Horizontal means in the same direction as the horizon, which is the distant line where the land and sky seem to meet.

2 adjective
A horizontal line is a straight, level line going across, perpendicular to the vertical.

eg vertical ➡

horizontal

➡ perpendicular, vertical

hour noun

An hour is a measurement of time, lasting 60 minutes. There are 24 hours in a day.

eg There is one hour between these two times.

➡ time

hundredth

1 adjective
Hundredth (100th) is the ordinal number of a hundred.

eg On its hundredth throw the coin turned up heads.

2 noun
A hundredth is the fraction $\frac{1}{100}$.

eg A penny is a hundredth of a pound.

hypotenuse noun

The hypotenuse is the longest side of a right-angled triangle. It is the side opposite the right-angle.

eg hypotenuse

A B C D E F G **H** I J K L M N O P Q R S T U V W X Y Z

4|

I

I is the symbol which stands for 1 in the Roman number system.

eg III stands for 3.

➡ **Roman numerals**

icosahedron noun

An icosohedron is a 20-faced solid shape. All the faces of a regular icosahedron are equilateral triangles.

identical adjective

If two shapes, measures or numbers are exactly the same, they are identical.

eg These triangles are identical.

imperial system noun

The imperial system is a set of measuring units which was once used throughout the UK. The system includes measures of length, such as yards, feet and inches; measures of weight, such as pounds and ounces; and measures of capacity, such as gallons and pints.

eg A yard is 3 feet and is approximately 1 metre in length.

➡ **metric system**

impossible adjective

If an event is impossible, it cannot happen.

eg On the probability scale the chance of an impossible event is 0.

➡ **probability**

improper fraction noun

1234

An improper fraction is a fraction that has a numerator greater than the denominator. Its value is greater than 1.

eg $\frac{9}{4}$ is an improper fraction and is the same as the mixed number $2\frac{1}{4}$.

➡ **denominator, fraction, mixed number, numerator**

inch noun

An inch is a unit of length in the imperial system. There are 12 inches in 1 foot.

🛈 An inch was originally defined by Edward II. It was the length of three barley grains end to end.

eg

1 inch

➡ **imperial system, foot**

increase verb

+√x⁻÷

If you increase something you make it more or larger.

eg If you increase a number by 15 you add 15 to it.

➡ **decrease**

index (plural: indices) noun

1234

The index is the small digit to the top right of a number which tells you the number of times the number is multiplied by itself. The index can also be called the power.

eg $4^3 = 4 \times 4 \times 4 = 64$. The index is 3.

➡ **square number**

infinity (∞) noun

1234

Infinity is a quantity larger than any known quantity.

eg If you count for ever there will always be a bigger number than the last one you counted, so infinity is never-ending.

integer noun

1234

An integer is another name for a whole number. It includes positive and negative numbers. Zero is also an integer.

eg –5, –3, 0, 4 and 7 are all integers.

➡ **whole number**

interpret verb

To interpret is to explain and describe something.

eg You interpret a graph by looking at it and describing the results that it shows.

A
B
C
D
E
F
G
H
I
J
K
L
M
N
O
P
Q
R
S
T
U
V
W
X
Y
Z

interrogate verb

To interrogate a database is to explore its contents.

eg You need to interrogate a database on birds to find out different wing-spans.

intersection noun

An intersection is a crossing point or place. Two lines intersect at a point.

eg intersection

interval noun

An interval is a period of time. It can also mean the difference between two numbers.

eg There is an interval of 5 between the numbers 4 and 9.

inverse noun

The inverse is the reverse or opposite of something.

$+\sqrt{x}-\div$

eg Addition is the inverse of subtraction.

irregular adjective

Irregular objects do not follow a given pattern or format.

eg
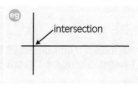

75°

40°   65°

This scalene triangle is irregular because it has three different angles and sides of different lengths.

➡ regular

isosceles triangle noun

An isosceles triangle has two equal sides with the opposite angles also equal.

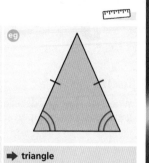

The word isosceles comes from two Greek words, *isos* meaning equal and *skelos* meaning leg.

➡ **triangle**

Jj

justify verb

????

When you justify a decision you provide good reasons to support it.

eg You must give evidence to justify your conclusions.

kilo- prefix

Kilo- is a prefix meaning 1000.

A kilometre is 1000 metres.

kilogram (kg) noun

A kilogram is a measurement of weight or mass in the metric system, equal to 1000 grams.

A bag of sugar weighs about 1 kilogram.

➡ gram

kilometre (km) noun

A kilometre is a measurement of length in the metric system, equal to 1000 metres.

It takes about 10 minutes to walk 1 kilometre.

➡ metre

kite noun

A kite is a 4-sided flat shape with two pairs of equal adjacent sides. One pair of opposite angles are equal and the diagonals of a kite intersect at right-angles.

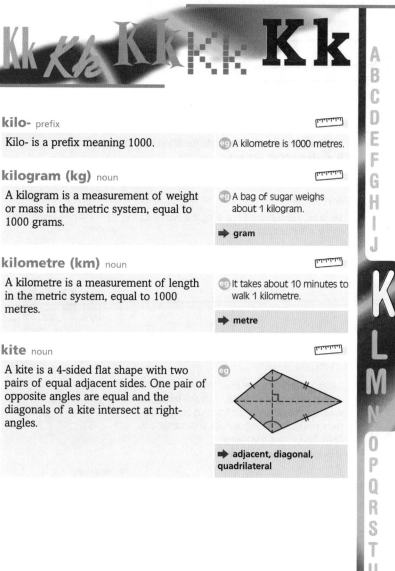

➡ adjacent, diagonal, quadrilateral

L

L is the symbol which stands for 50 in the Roman number system.

eg LV is 55.

➡ **Roman numerals**

label verb

To label something is to give it a name to show information.

eg Each axis on a graph needs a label.

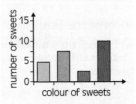

latitude noun

Lines of latitude are imaginary circles drawn around the Earth, parallel to the equator. Together with lines of longitude they make a grid on the Earth's surface to help find exact positions.

lines of latitude

➡ **longitude**

LCD ➡ **lowest common denominator**

LCM ➡ **lowest common multiple**

leap year noun

A leap year is a calendar year of 366 days, with February having 29 days instead of 28. A leap year occurs every fourth year.

eg 2002 was not a leap year, but 2000 was, because the year is divisible by 4.

A leap year is needed because the length of a year is approximately $365\frac{1}{4}$ days. The four quarter days are added together to make an extra day every four years.

➡ **year**

least adjective

?　?　?　?

The least amount is the smallest quantity.

eg A graph of favourite colours of a group of children will show the least popular colour.

length noun

Length is the distance between two points or the two ends of a line.
A length of time is the amount of time from the start of an event to its finish.

eg

The length of this line is 3 cm.

➡ breadth, width

less than (<) phrase

1 2 3 4

If one quantity is smaller than another, the first is less than the second.

eg 0.35 < 0.5
This shows that 0.35 is less than 0.5.

➡ greater than

likelihood noun

The likelihood of something happening is the chance or probability of it happening.

eg The likelihood of getting a 3 when throwing a 1–6 dice is a 1 in 6 chance.

➡ chance, probability

likely adjective

If an event is likely there is a good chance it will happen.

eg It is likely that you will get out of bed tomorrow.

➡ even chance, possible, unlikely

line noun

A line is a straight or curved length with no width. A line drawn on paper always has a very narrow width, but even if it is quite thick it is still called a line.

eg This is a curved line.

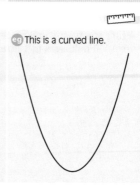

A B C D E F G H I J K L M N O P Q R S T U V W X Y Z

line graph noun

A line graph is a graph where all the points are joined by straight lines.

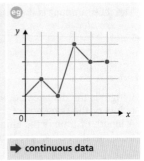

➡ **continuous data**

line of symmetry noun

A line of symmetry is a line about which a shape is symmetrical. If the shape is folded along the line, one half fits exactly over the other half.

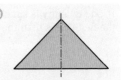

➡ **line symmetry, mirror line, reflection, symmetry**

line symmetry noun

A shape has line symmetry or reflection symmetry when two or more of its parts are matching shapes. If a mirror is placed along the line separating the two matching shapes, the shape looks unchanged.

➡ **line of symmetry, mirror line, reflection, symmetry**

litre (l) noun

A litre is a metric unit of capacity. There are 1000 millilitres in 1 litre.

A normal glass holds about one-third of a litre.

1 litre

➡ **capacity, millilitre**

longitude noun

Longitude is the distance in degrees east or west of the Greenwich Meridian at 0°. Lines of longitude are imaginary circles drawn around the Earth. Each line passes through the North and South poles. Together with lines of latitude they make a grid on the Earth's surface to help find exact positions.

lines of
longitude

➡ latitude

loss noun

In business, to make a loss is to lose money on a deal and therefore not make a profit.

A garage made a loss last month because they bought some cars for more than they sold them.

➡ profit

lowest common denominator (LCD) noun

The lowest common denominator is the lowest common multiple of all the denominators in a set of fractions.

To put these in order of size, work out the LCD.
$\frac{2}{3}, \frac{3}{4}, \frac{1}{6}$.
12 is the lowest common denominator of 3, 4 and 6:
$\frac{2}{3} = \frac{8}{12}, \frac{3}{4} = \frac{9}{12}, \frac{1}{6} = \frac{1}{12}$
So the order is $\frac{1}{6}, \frac{2}{3}, \frac{3}{4}$.

➡ denominator

lowest common multiple (LCM) noun

The lowest common multiple is the lowest number which is a multiple of two or more numbers.

The lowest common multiple of 3, 6 and 8 is 24.

➡ multiple

A B C D E F G H I J K L M N O P Q R S T U V W X Y Z

lowest terms noun

1234

If a fraction is in its lowest terms, it has been cancelled until it is in its simplest form. The only common factor of both the numerator and denominator is 1.

eg $\frac{15}{20}$ in its lowest terms is $\frac{3}{4}$.

➡ cancel, denominator, numerator, reduce, simplify

lozenge ➡ rhombus

M

1234

M is the symbol which stands for 1000 in the Roman number system.

eg MCM stands for 1900. This means 1000 plus 100 less than 1000, which is 1900.

➡ **Roman numerals**

magic square noun

1234

A magic square is an arrangement of numbers in a square. If you add together all the numbers in any row, column or diagonal, the answer is the same.

🔴 Some Ancient Chinese and Arabic mathematicians believed that these number squares had magic powers.

eg

6	1	8
7	5	3
2	9	4

majority noun

1234

A majority of a group is more than half the items or people in that group.

eg In a survey about vegetables, the majority of the people preferred carrots to cabbage.

➡ **minority**

mapping noun

????

A mapping changes something by following a given rule. Arrows are usually used to show a mapping.

eg The mappings 2 → 6, 5 → 15 and 8 → 24 have the rule 'multiply by 3'.

mass noun

The mass of an object is the amount of material contained in it. The more massive an object is, the harder it is to make it move. In the metric system mass is measured in grams and kilograms.

🔴 On Earth your mass and weight are the same, but weight is effected by the pull of gravity. Your mass on the moon would be the same as on earth but your weight would be different.

eg

2.00 kg

This pumpkin has a mass of 2 kg.

➡ **weight**

mathematics noun

? ? ?

Mathematics is the study of numbers, patterns and shapes. We use mathematics to help solve many different kinds of problems.

eg Mathematics includes many topics, such as numbers, calculations, algebra, shape, measures and handling data.

maximum noun

1 2 3 4

The maximum is the largest or greatest value or number in a set of numbers.

eg The maximum total with three 1–6 dice is 18.

➡ **minimum**

mean noun

The mean, or arithmetic mean, of a set of numbers is one way of working out an average. The mean is found by totalling all the numbers and dividing by how many numbers there are altogether.

eg The mean of 3, 6, 8 and 7 is 6.
$(3 + 6 + 8 + 7) \div 4 = 6$

➡ **average, median, mode**

measure verb

To measure something is to find the size, quantity or degree of it.

eg Tom measured the height of the gate.

➡ **angle, area, capacity, length, mass**

measurement noun

A measurement is an amount or size discovered by measuring.

eg The exact measurement of the mass of the parcel was 2.7 kg.

➡ **angle, area, capacity, length, mass**

median noun

The median is the middle number in a set of numbers. It is one way of working out an average. The median is found by arranging all the numbers in order and finding the middle number.

eg To find the median of 41 cm, 28 cm, 52 cm, 31 cm and 29 cm, write them in order:
28 cm, 29 cm, 31 cm, 41 cm, 52 cm.

The middle number, 31 cm, is the median.

➡ **average, mean, mode**

mega- prefix

Mega- is a prefix meaning 1 000 000.

eg Computer memory size can be measured in megabytes. A megabyte is just over one million bytes.

method noun

A method is a description of the way of doing a calculation or solving a problem.

eg There are several mental methods for working out 39 + 84.

metre (m) noun

A metre is a measurement of length in the metric system.
There are 100 centimetres in 1 metre.

eg A long stride is about one metre long.

➡ centimetre, kilometre, length

metric system noun

The metric system is a system of weights and measures. All the units in the metric system are in tens, hundreds and thousands.

The metric system was developed in France in the 18th Century. In 1897 a law was passed in the UK giving permission to use metric weights and measures.

eg Millimetres, metres, litres, grams and kilograms are all examples of units in the metric system.

➡ imperial system

midday noun

Midday is 12 o'clock in the middle of the day. Another word for midday is noon.

eg Between midnight and midday, the time using the 12-hour clock is a.m. After midday up to midnight the time is p.m.

➡ a.m., p.m.

midnight noun

Midnight is 12 o'clock in the middle of the night.

eg The video was set to record a film starting at midnight and finishing at 2.10 a.m.

A B C D E F G H I J K L M N O P Q R S T U V W X Y Z

55

mile noun

A mile is an imperial measurement of length. There are 1760 yards in one mile.

The word mile comes from the Latin word *mille*, meaning one thousand. A mile was said to be the distance of 1000 paces.

eg The one mile race is four laps of a 400 metre track.

➡ imperial system

millennium noun

A millennium is a period of 1000 years.

eg We are now in the third millennium, which started on 1st January 2001.

milli- prefix

Milli- is a prefix meaning $\frac{1}{1000}$.

eg A millilitre is one-thousandth of a litre.

➡ centi-

millilitre (ml) noun

A millilitre is a measurement of capacity equal to $\frac{1}{1000}$ litre. There are 1000 ml in 1 litre.

eg 1 millilitre is a tiny amount. A teaspoon holds about 5 ml of liquid.

➡ capacity, litre

million noun

A million is the number 1 000 000. It is a very large number. If you counted to 1 million with a number every second, it would take you over 11 days.

eg A million is one thousand thousand.

minimum noun

The minimum is the smallest or lowest value or number in a set of numbers.

eg The minimum temperature reached last night was 2° C.

➡ maximum

minority noun

A minority of a group is fewer than half the items or people in that group.

eg A minority of players voted to change the colour of the football kit, so it remained blue.

➡ majority

minus (−) preposition

1234

You use minus to show that one number is being subtracted from another.

eg 13 minus 7 is 6.

🔸 Minus is also sometimes used to say negative numbers, such as minus 5 for −5. It is actually better to say negative 5 so that it is not confused with the operation of subtraction. But we do use minus for temperatures. If the temperature is five degrees below zero we say that it is minus five degrees.

➡ **subtraction, take away**

minute noun

A minute is a length of time. There are 60 seconds in one minute and 60 minutes in one hour.

eg The second hand takes one minute to go around the watch once.

mirror line noun

A mirror line is another name for a line of symmetry and is a line about which a shape is symmetrical. If a mirror is placed on the line, the half shape and its reflection show the whole shape.

eg

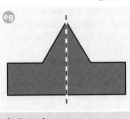

➡ **line of symmetry, reflection, symmetry**

mixed number noun

1234

A mixed number, or mixed fraction, is a whole number together with a proper fraction.

eg $3\frac{2}{5}$ is a mixed number.

➡ **improper fraction**

Möbius strip noun

A Möbius strip is a flat strip of paper which is twisted halfway and the ends joined together. The shape is special as it has only one side and one edge.

The Möbius strip was invented in the 19th Century by August Möbius, a German mathematician.
Try making a Möbius strip and prove it only has one side by drawing a line along the centre of the strip without lifting your pen – you will eventually come back to your starting point.

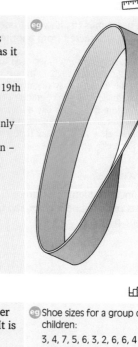

mode noun

The mode is the most common number or item in a set of numbers or items. It is one way of finding an average.

Shoe sizes for a group of children:

3, 4, 7, 5, 6, 3, 2, 6, 6, 4

The mode for these shoe sizes is size 6.

➡ average, mean, median

month noun

A month has between 28 and 31 days and is approximately four weeks. It is the time it takes for the moon to go around the Earth once.

The length of a month is approximately equal to the time between one New Moon and the next New Moon which is 29.5 days.

In the Gregorian calendar, used by most people in the world, there are 12 months in a year.

➡ day, leap year, year

multiple noun

A multiple is a number made by multiplying together two other numbers. If one number divides exactly into another number, the second is a multiple of the first.

15 is a multiple of 5 because 3 × 5 is 15.

All multiples of 5 end in 0 or 5.

➡ common multiple

multiplication (×) noun

$+\sqrt{x}-\div$

Multiplication is the operation of adding a number to itself a given number of times. With multiplication you multiply two numbers together. Changing the order does not matter as the answer stays the same – six lots of three (3 × 6) is equal to three lots of six (6 × 3).

eg Learning your multiplication tables helps to speed up calculations.

multiply verb

$+\sqrt{x}-\div$

To multiply is to add a number to itself a given number of times.

eg To multiply 4 by 5 means to find out what 5 lots of 4 equals.

$4 \times 5 = 20$

A
B
C
D
E
F
G
H
I
J
K
L
M
N
O
P
Q
R
S
T
U
V
W
X
Y
Z

narrow adjective

Narrow means thin, or of small width.

eg Sam cut a narrow strip from a piece of card, 1.5 cm wide.

➡ width

natural number noun

1 2 3 4

Natural numbers are the set of positive numbers, as used in counting. Zero can be included or not – it is a matter of choice.

eg 1, 2, 3, 4, 5, 6 … are all natural numbers.

➡ integer, whole number

nautical mile noun

A nautical mile is a measurement of length used at sea. It is equal to 1852 metres.

eg 1 knot is a unit of speed of one nautical mile per hour.

nearest adjective, preposition

1 2 3 4

The nearest is the closest whole number or multiple of ten, used when rounding.

eg 38.7 is 39 rounded to the nearest whole number.

➡ round

negative number noun

1 2 3 4

A number less than zero is a negative number. The minus sign (–) is used to show when a number is negative.

eg –14, –8, and –25 are all negative numbers.

➡ minus, positive number

net noun

A net is a flat shape that you can fold up to make into a solid shape.

eg This is a net of a cube.

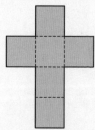

nonagon noun

A nonagon is a flat shape with nine straight sides.

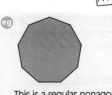

This is a regular nonagon.

➡ **polygon**

north noun

North is one of the four main points of the compass, opposite to south.

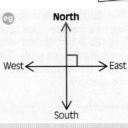

➡ **compass, east, south, west**

nought noun

1234

Nought is an old word meaning nothing or zero. It is written as the digit 0. Nowadays we use zero more often in mathematics.

eg If you take seven away from seven you are left with nought.

➡ **zero**

number noun

1234

A number is a symbol used for counting.

eg We use the digits 0, 1, 2, 3, 4, 5, 6, 7, 8 and 9 to make our numbers.

➡ **digit**

number bond noun

$+\sqrt{x^-}\div$

Number bonds are pairs of numbers that make a particular total.

eg The number bonds for 8 are 0 + 8, 1 + 7, 2 + 6, 3 + 5 and 4 + 4.

number line noun

1234

A number line is a line with a scale showing numbers in order.

eg

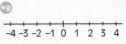

-4 -3 -2 -1 0 1 2 3 4

number sentence noun

$+\sqrt{x}-\div$

A number sentence is a statement used in mathematics which has numbers instead of words.

eg 4 + 8 = 12 is a number sentence.

numeral noun

1 2 3 4

A numeral is a word or a figure written down to stand for a number.

eg Five, 5 and V are all numerals.

numerator noun

1 2 3 4

The numerator is the number above the line in a fraction. The number below the line, the denominator, shows you the number of equal parts. The numerator tells you how many of these equal parts you are using.

eg In the fraction $\frac{3}{4}$, the numerator is 3.
$\frac{3}{4}$ of 20 is 15.
$(20 \div 4) \times 3 = 15$.

➡ **denominator, fraction**

Oo

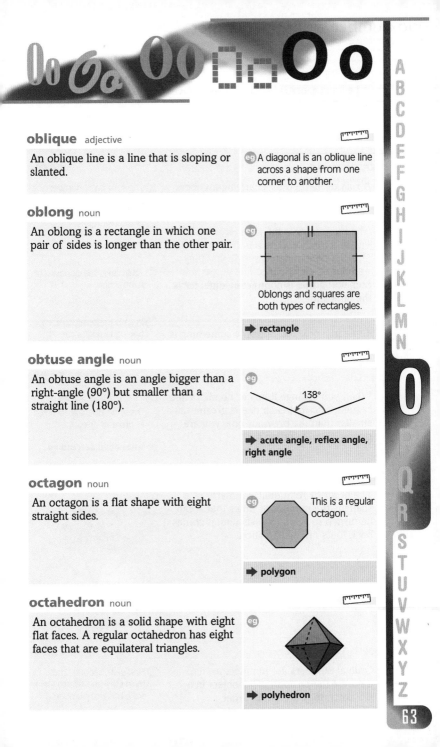

oblique adjective

An oblique line is a line that is sloping or slanted.

eg A diagonal is an oblique line across a shape from one corner to another.

oblong noun

An oblong is a rectangle in which one pair of sides is longer than the other pair.

eg

Oblongs and squares are both types of rectangles.

➡ rectangle

obtuse angle noun

An obtuse angle is an angle bigger than a right-angle (90°) but smaller than a straight line (180°).

eg 138°

➡ acute angle, reflex angle, right angle

octagon noun

An octagon is a flat shape with eight straight sides.

eg This is a regular octagon.

➡ polygon

octahedron noun

An octahedron is a solid shape with eight flat faces. A regular octahedron has eight faces that are equilateral triangles.

eg

➡ polyhedron

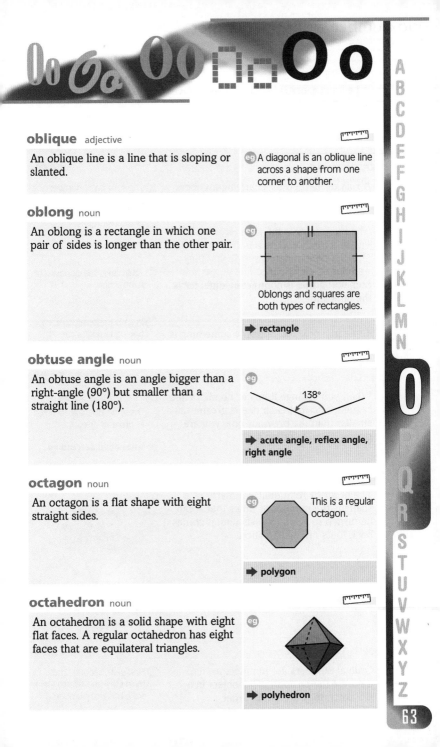

odd number noun

1234

When a number is divided by 2 and gives a remainder of 1, it is an odd number.

eg All odd numbers end with the digits 1, 3, 5, 7 or 9. So 4027 is an odd number.

➡ even number

operation noun

+√x⁻÷

A rule or method for changing numbers in a calculation is an operation.

eg The four basic number operations are addition, subtraction, multiplication and division.

opposite

1 noun
Something that is completely different is the opposite.

eg Addition is the opposite of subtraction.

2 preposition
To be in a position opposite something is to be facing it.

eg In an isosceles triangle, the two equal angles are opposite the two equal sides.

order noun

1234

When you arrange items or numbers in a sequence so that each one is greater or smaller than the previous one, you are putting them in order.

eg 17, 21, 28, 31, 42, 44
These numbers are written in order of size.

➡ ascending, descending

order of rotational symmetry noun

The order of rotational symmetry of a shape is the number of times that it can be turned to fit on to itself until it comes back to its original position.

eg

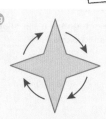

This star has an order of rotational symmetry of 4.

ordinal number noun

1234

Ordinal numbers are numbers used to describe the position of an object in a set, when they are put in order.

eg First (1st), second (2nd), third (3rd) and fourth (4th) are all ordinal numbers.

origin noun

The origin is the point on a graph where the two axes cross. The coordinates for the origin are (0,0).

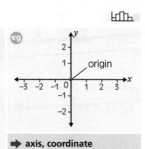

➡ **axis, coordinate**

ounce (oz) noun

An ounce is an imperial unit of mass or weight. There are 16 ounces in a pound (lb).

eg A slice of bread weighs about two ounces.

➡ **imperial system, pound**

outcome noun

Outcomes are possible results of a probability experiment.

eg If you roll a 1–6 dice the possible outcomes are any of the numbers from 1 to 6.

oval noun

An oval is a flat egg-shape or an ellipse.

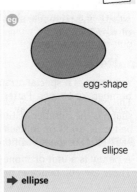

egg-shape

ellipse

➡ **ellipse**

Pp

pair noun

1 2 3 4

A pair is a set of two things.

eg A trapezium has a pair of parallel sides.

palindrome noun

1 2 3 4

A palindrome is a number that is the same when it is read forwards as it is when it is read backwards. A word can also be palindromic, such as 'level'.

eg 28182 and 34543 are both palindromes.

parallel adjective

Lines that are parallel always stay the same distance apart and never meet.

eg A rhombus has two pairs of parallel sides.

parallelogram noun

A parallelogram is a quadrilateral with two pairs of parallel sides. The opposite sides are also equal in length. A rhombus, square and rectangle are all special types of parallelograms.

eg

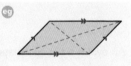

pattern noun

? ? ? ?

A pattern is a special arrangement of numbers or shapes. Patterns repeat or change in a regular way.

eg 0, 5, 10, 15, 20, 25, 30 ... The five times table has a special pattern.

penny (p) (plural: pence) noun

1 2 3 4

A penny is a unit of money in the UK. There are 100 pence in one pound.

eg This costs 34 pence.

➡ **pound**

pentagon noun

A pentagon is a flat shape with five straight sides.

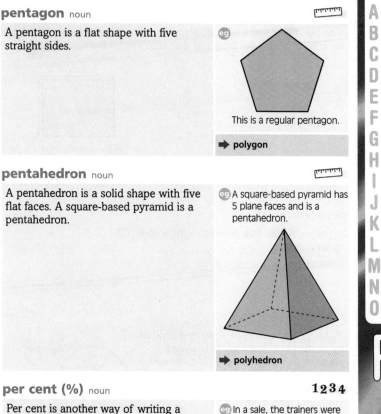

This is a regular pentagon.

➡ **polygon**

pentahedron noun

A pentahedron is a solid shape with five flat faces. A square-based pyramid is a pentahedron.

A square-based pyramid has 5 plane faces and is a pentahedron.

➡ **polyhedron**

per cent (%) noun

Per cent is another way of writing a fraction out of 100.
One hundred per cent (100%) is the whole, 50% is the same as $\frac{50}{100}$ or $\frac{1}{2}$.

In a sale, the trainers were reduced by 50% from £42 to £21.

➡ **fraction, percentage**

percentage noun

Percentage is a fraction out of 100. You divide something into 100 parts to make a percentage.

The percentage of diamonds in a pack of cards is one quarter or 25%.

➡ **fraction, per cent**

perfect number noun

A number that is the sum of its factors (apart from itself) is a perfect number.

6 is a perfect number as
$1 + 2 + 3 = 6$.
28 is a perfect number as
$1 + 2 + 4 + 7 + 14 = 28$.

67

perimeter noun

The perimeter is the edge or boundary of an area. It is also the length of that edge.

The perimeter of a rectangle is found by adding the lengths of all the sides.

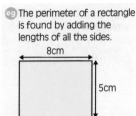

The perimeter is 8 cm + 8 cm + 5 cm + 5 cm = 26 cm.

➡ area

perpendicular adjective

A perpendicular line is one at right angles to another line.

pi (π) noun

If the circumference of a circle is divided by its diameter, the answer is always equal to pi. It is just over 3, but can never be worked out exactly. It is approximately 3.1415926 but the digits after the decimal point go on for ever.

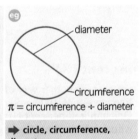

π = circumference ÷ diameter

➡ circle, circumference, diameter

pictogram noun

A chart using pictures or symbols to represent numbers of items is a pictogram or pictograph. Each symbol stands for a certain number of items. The meaning of the symbols is shown by a key.

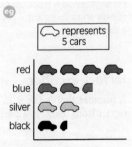

pie chart noun

A pie chart is a circular chart that shows how something is shared out or divided up.

 This pie chart shows that most of the cars passing the school were red.

Colours of cars

pint (pt) noun

A pint is an imperial unit of capacity. There are eight pints in 1 gallon.

Milk bottles hold 1 pint of milk.

➡ **gallon, imperial system**

place value noun

1234

The place value is the position or place of a digit in a number. The same digit has a different value at different places in the number.

In the number 384, the place value of 3 is 300, 8 is 80 and 4 is 4.

$300 + 80 + 4 = 384$

➡ **digit**

plan noun

A plan is a scale drawing or design for an object or building.

This is the plan for a new office.

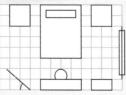

plane noun

A plane is a flat surface. Plane shapes are flat shapes with length and width but no thickness. They are two-dimensional shapes.

eg This is a plane shape.

➡ two-dimensional

plot verb

When you plot points on a graph you mark the position of given coordinates.

eg Position (3,4) has been plotted.

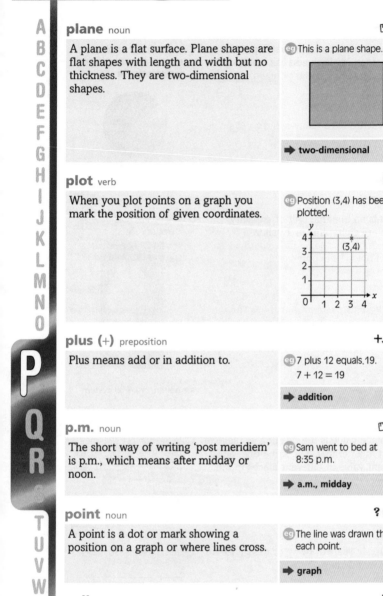

plus (+) preposition

Plus means add or in addition to.

eg 7 plus 12 equals 19.
$7 + 12 = 19$

➡ addition

p.m. noun

The short way of writing 'post meridiem' is p.m., which means after midday or noon.

eg Sam went to bed at 8:35 p.m.

➡ a.m., midday

point noun

A point is a dot or mark showing a position on a graph or where lines cross.

eg The line was drawn through each point.

➡ graph

poll noun

A poll is a survey of people's opinions or intentions.

eg The poll showed that more people preferred going on holiday to a hot place than to a cold place.

polygon noun

A polygon is a flat or plane shape with many sides. If a polygon has equal sides it is said to be a regular polygon.

eg A square and equilateral triangle are examples of regular polygons.

polyhedron (plural: polyhedra) noun

A polyhedron is a many-sided solid shape with flat sides.

eg

population noun

The number of people that live in a certain place is its population.

eg The population of the UK is approximately 60 million.

portion noun

A portion is a piece or part of a whole.

eg If a cake is divided into five equal portions, each portion is $\frac{1}{5}$ of the whole.

position

1 noun
The position of an object is its place or location. Position can also mean the order in which things are placed.

eg The top three positions in a race are 1st, 2nd and 3rd.

2 verb
When you put something in a certain place you position it.

eg Emma positioned the pieces on the board to begin the game of chess.

positive number noun

A number greater than zero is a positive number. The plus sign (+) is sometimes used to show when a number is positive.

eg 3, 18 and 40 are all positive numbers.

➡ negative number

possible adjective

If an event is possible it means it can happen.

eg It is possible that the sun will shine for at least three days next week.

➡ chance, likely, unlikely

A B C D E F G H I J K L M N O P Q R S T U V W X Y Z

pound

1 noun

A pound (lb) is an imperial unit of weight or mass. There are 16 ounces in a pound and 14 pounds in a stone.

eg Four apples weigh about a pound.

2 noun

A pound (£) is also a unit of money in the UK. 100 pence equal £1.

eg Three packets of crisps cost about £1.

➡ **ounce, penny, stone**

power ➡ index

predict verb

If you predict, you forecast that an event will occur.

eg If you tossed a coin 100 times, you could predict that it will show heads 50 times.

price noun

The price of something is its cost or expense.

eg In a sale, the price of a tennis racket was reduced to £15.

prime factor noun

A prime factor is a factor that is a prime number.

eg The factors of 12 are 1, 2, 3, 4, 6 and 12. The prime factors are 2 and 3.

➡ **factor, prime number**

prime number noun

A prime number is any whole number, apart from 1, that can only be divided by itself and by 1 without leaving a remainder. Another way of saying this is that a prime number only has two factors, 1 and itself.

eg The first four prime numbers are 2, 3, 5 and 7.

➡ **factor**

prism noun

A prism is a solid shape with matching ends. The ends are polygons, such as triangles, squares or hexagons. A prism has the same cross-section all the way along its length.

eg A hexagonal prism.

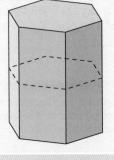

➡ **cross-section, polygon**

probability noun

The probability of an event happening is the chance it may happen, which can be given as a fraction, a decimal or a percentage.

eg The probability of throwing a 6 with a 1–6 dice is 1 in 6 or $\frac{1}{6}$.

➡ **certain, chance, likelihood, probability scale**

probability scale noun

A probability scale is an ordered line numbered from 0, which is the probability of an impossible event, to 1, which is the probability of a certain event. All probabilities lie between 0 and 1.

eg

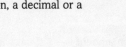

➡ **certain, chance, likelihood, probability**

probable adjective

If an event is probable it is likely to happen.

eg It is probable that the temperatures in July will be above 15°C.

product noun

When two or more numbers are multiplied together, the answer is the product of those numbers.

eg The product of 3 and 5 is 15 $(3 \times 5 = 15)$.

➡ **multiply**

profit noun

1234

In business, to make a profit is to make money on a deal.

> A profit was made when they sold the house because they sold it for more money than they bought it.

➡ loss

proper fraction noun

1234

A proper fraction has a value less than 1. The numerator is smaller than the denominator.

> $\frac{7}{8}$ is a proper fraction.

➡ denominator, fraction, numerator, unit fraction

property noun

????

A property of a shape or number is a particular fact or feature of it that makes it part of a group with the same properties.

> It is a property of square numbers that they have an odd number of factors.

proportion noun

1234

Finding the proportion of an amount is the same as finding the fraction of the whole amount. A proportion can be written as a fraction.

The proportion of squares that are red is $\frac{6}{10}$ or $\frac{3}{5}$.

➡ fraction, ratio

protractor noun

A protractor is an instrument used for measuring angles. It has a scale that is marked in degrees.

➡ angle, degree

pyramid noun

A pyramid is a solid shape with triangular faces. The faces meet at a point called a vertex. The base of a pyramid can be any polygon, such as a triangle, a square or a hexagon.

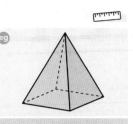

➡ polygon, polyhedron, vertex

quadrant

1 noun
A quadrant is one-quarter of a circle.

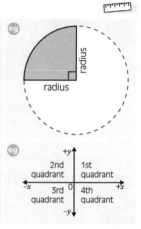

2 noun
A quadrant is also the name given to each of the four areas on a graph or coordinates grid. The graph is divided into four quadrants by its axes.

quadrilateral noun

A quadrilateral is a flat or plane shape with four straight sides.

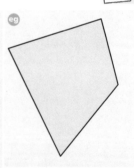

➡ arrowhead, kite, parallelogram, polygon, rectangle, rhombus, square, trapezium

quadruple

1234

1 verb
When you quadruple something you multiply it by four.

If you have £6 and it is quadrupled, you will have £24.

2 adjective
Four times a number is its quadruple.

24 is the quadruple of 6.

quarter noun

1 2 3 4

A quarter is one of four equal parts. One-quarter ($\frac{1}{4}$) is one-fourth part of a whole.

$\frac{1}{4}$	$\frac{1}{4}$
$\frac{1}{4}$	$\frac{1}{4}$

➡ fraction

questionnaire noun

A questionnaire is a sheet of questions used to collect data.

The class made up a questionnaire about the leisure activities of the pupils in their school.

quotient noun

$+\sqrt{}\times\div$

A quotient is the number of times that one number will divide into another number. It is the whole number part of the answer to a division calculation.

When you divide 9 by 2, the quotient is 4.

$9 \div 2 = 4.5$

➡ division

A B C D E F G H I J K L M N O P Q R S T U V W X Y Z

Rr

radius (plural radii) noun

The radius is the length of a straight line from the centre of a circle to its circumference.

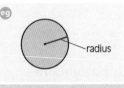

➡ circle, circumference, diameter

random adjective

Random means purely by chance. A random sample is a selection where each sample has an equal chance of being picked.

eg The numbers in a lottery are chosen at random so they have an equal chance of coming up each week.

➡ chance, likelihood, probability

range noun

The range is the spread of data; it is the difference between the greatest and least values.

eg The heights of a group of children ranged from 132 cm to 154 cm. The range was 22 cm.

➡ average, median, mean, mode

ratio noun

1234

Ratio compares one part or amount with another.

The ratio of white to red squares is 4 to 6 or 2 to 3. For every 2 white squares there are 3 red squares. This is written as 2:3.

➡ proportion

rectangle noun

A rectangle is a four-sided flat shape. It has two pairs of opposite, equal parallel sides and each angle is a right angle (90°).

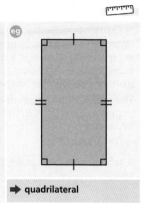

➡ **quadrilateral**

recurring adjective

1234

Recurring means repeating. A recurring decimal has digits that are in a continuous pattern, like 0.33333 … or 0.252525 … .

On your calculator, the calculation 2 ÷ 3 gives the answer 0.6666666. This is 'zero point six recurring' which is sometimes written as 0.6̇.

➡ **decimal**

reduce verb

1234

To reduce is to make smaller in size. A fraction is reduced by cancelling or simplifying it to its lowest terms.

$\frac{12}{18}$ is reduced to $\frac{2}{3}$ in its lowest terms.

➡ **cancel, lowest terms, simplify**

reflection noun

A reflection is an image seen in a mirror. A shape with two sides that are mirror images has reflection or line symmetry.

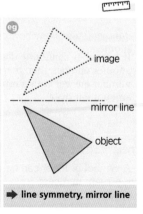

image

mirror line

object

➡ **line symmetry, mirror line**

reflective symmetry noun

A shape has reflective symmetry or line symmetry when two or more of its parts are matching shapes. If a mirror is placed along the line separating the two matching shapes, the shape looks unchanged.

➡ line symmetry

reflex angle noun

A reflex angle is an angle greater than 180°.

eg 320°

➡ acute angle, obtuse angle

regular adjective

A regular polygon has sides of equal length and angles of equal size.

eg These are all regular polygons.

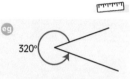

➡ irregular, polygon

relationship noun

1234

When you look for a relationship between sets of numbers, you look for the way they are connected, often with a rule.

eg 3 → 6, 8 → 16, 5 → 10
The relationship arrows all show 'is half of'.

➡ function

remainder noun

+√x⁻÷

If a number cannot be divided exactly by another number, then there is a whole number answer with a remainder or an amount left over.

eg When you divide 23 by 4, the quotient is 5 with a remainder of 3.
23 ÷ 4 = 5 remainder 3

➡ division, quotient

represent verb

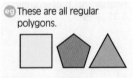

A symbol or letter can be used to represent numbers.

eg In the formula Area = l × b, l represents length and b represents breadth.

revolution noun

A revolution is a complete turn through 360°.

eg Four right angles make one complete revolution.

➡ right angle

rhombus noun

A rhombus is a special parallelogram. It is a flat shape with four equal sides but no right angles. It is sometimes called a lozenge or a diamond.

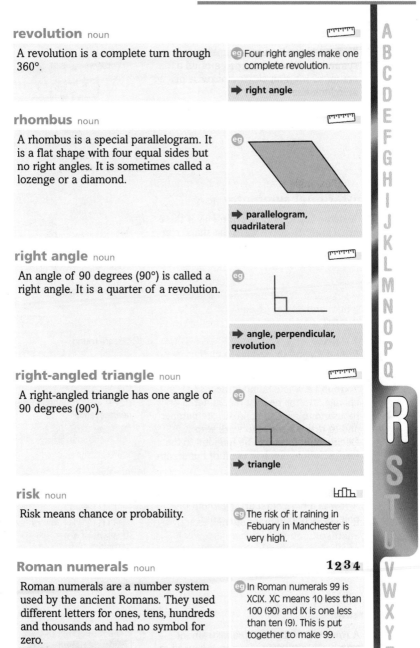

➡ parallelogram, quadrilateral

right angle noun

An angle of 90 degrees (90°) is called a right angle. It is a quarter of a revolution.

➡ angle, perpendicular, revolution

right-angled triangle noun

A right-angled triangle has one angle of 90 degrees (90°).

➡ triangle

risk noun

Risk means chance or probability.

eg The risk of it raining in Febuary in Manchester is very high.

Roman numerals noun

1234

Roman numerals are a number system used by the ancient Romans. They used different letters for ones, tens, hundreds and thousands and had no symbol for zero.

eg In Roman numerals 99 is XCIX. XC means 10 less than 100 (90) and IX is one less than ten (9). This is put together to make 99.

➡ C, D, I, L, M, V, X

A B C D E F G H I J K L M N O P Q R S T U V W X Y Z

rotate verb

To rotate is to turn around. When a shape is rotated it is turned around a centre of rotation either clockwise or anticlockwise.

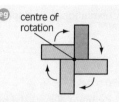

eg centre of rotation

➡ **centre of rotation, rotational symmetry**

rotational symmetry noun

A shape has rotational symmetry if there are a number of positions the shape can take when rotated, and still look the same.

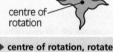

centre of rotation

➡ **centre of rotation, rotate**

round

1 adjective
Round means shaped like a circle.

eg CDs are round.

2 verb
To round a whole number means to change it to the nearest ten, hundred or thousand to give an approximate number and to make it easier to work with. Decimal numbers can be rounded to the nearest whole number, tenth or hundredth.

eg 74 684 is 75 000 rounded to the nearest 1000.
8.2791 is 8.3 rounded to the nearest tenth.

row noun

1234

A row is a horizontal arrangement of objects or numbers going across.

eg

1	2	3	4
5	6	7	8
9	10	11	12

The numbers in the middle row are 5, 6, 7 and 8.

➡ **column**

ruler noun

A ruler is a straight-edged instrument with a scale marked along it. It is used to draw and measure straight lines.

eg

scale

1 noun

A scale is a marked measuring line.

eg If you read the scale you will see that this jug has 600 ml of liquid in it.

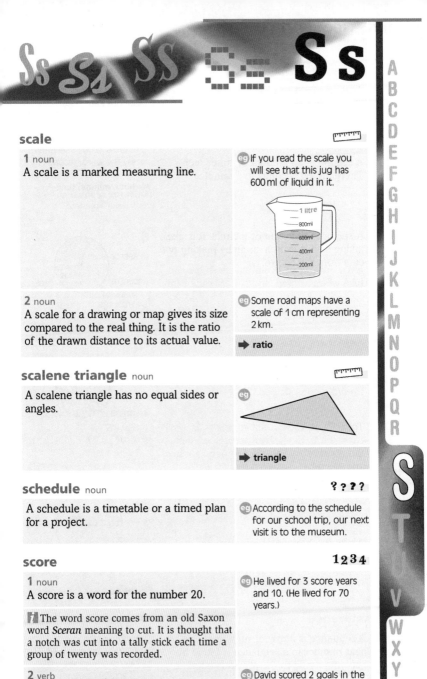

2 noun

A scale for a drawing or map gives its size compared to the real thing. It is the ratio of the drawn distance to its actual value.

eg Some road maps have a scale of 1 cm representing 2 km.

➡ ratio

scalene triangle noun

A scalene triangle has no equal sides or angles.

eg

➡ triangle

schedule noun

? ? ? ?

A schedule is a timetable or a timed plan for a project.

eg According to the schedule for our school trip, our next visit is to the museum.

score

1 2 3 4

1 noun

A score is a word for the number 20.

🔲 The word score comes from an old Saxon word *Sceran* meaning to cut. It is thought that a notch was cut into a tally stick each time a group of twenty was recorded.

eg He lived for 3 score years and 10. (He lived for 70 years.)

2 verb

You score points or goals in games and sport.

eg David scored 2 goals in the football match.

second (2nd)

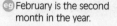

1 adjective
The second thing is the next thing after the first.

> February is the second month in the year.

➡ **first**

2 adjective
A second is an amount of time (sec). There are 60 seconds in 1 minute.

> It takes about 1 second to say the word 'second'.

➡ **hour, minute, time**

sector noun

A sector is a section of a circle. It is like taking a slice from a circle by making two cuts from the centre.

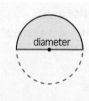

➡ **arc, radius**

segment noun

A segment of a circle is like a piece taken off the circle with a single cut.

➡ **circle**

semicircle noun

A semicircle is half a circle.

➡ **circle**

sequence noun

A sequence is a row of numbers. The next number in a sequence is found by applying a rule to the previous number.

> In the sequence 1, 5, 9, 13, 17, 21 … the rule is +4. The next two numbers will be 25 and 29.

➡ **Fibonacci sequence, pattern**

set noun

1 2 3 4

A set is a group of numbers, shapes or objects with a particular thing in common.

eg The set of odd numbers between 0 and 10 are 1, 3, 5, 7 and 9.

➡ **Carroll diagram, sort, Venn diagram**

set square noun

A set square is an instrument shaped like a right-angled triangle. It is used for drawing parallel and perpendicular lines.

➡ **parallel, perpendicular**

shape noun

A shape is a figure made up of drawn lines. In mathematics, shapes are drawn with lines to show their edges or sides. Plane shapes are flat, two-dimensional shapes and solid shapes are three-dimensional.

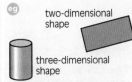

eg two-dimensional shape

three-dimensional shape

➡ **polygon, polyhedron, three-dimensional, two-dimensional**

share

1 2 3 4

1 noun

A share of something is a portion or part of a whole amount.

eg This pizza has been cut up into 6 shares.

2 verb

To share is to divide equally between two or more people.

eg If 24 sweets are shared equally between three people, each person will get eight sweets.

➡ **divide**

side noun

A side of a shape is the line that forms part of the edge or perimeter.

eg A square has four equal sides.

sign

1 noun
A sign is a symbol that shows the operation to use in a calculation.

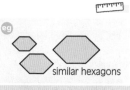

eg +, −, × and ÷ are the signs for addition, subtraction, multiplication and division.

2 noun
Sign also refers to the positive (+) or negative (−) value of a number.

eg −4 is less than zero and has a negative sign.

similar figure noun

Similar figures are figures that have the same shape but not the same size.

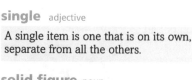

similar hexagons

➡ **congruent**

simplify verb

12**3**4

A fraction is simplified by reducing it to its lowest terms. Dividing the numerator and denominator by the same number will simplify a fraction.

eg $\frac{15}{21}$ can be simplified by dividing numerator and denominator by 3.
$\frac{15}{21} = \frac{5}{7}$

➡ **cancel, denominator, lowest terms, numerator, reduce**

single adjective

12**3**4

A single item is one that is on its own, separate from all the others.

eg There was a single apple left in the bowl.

solid figure noun

If an object has three dimensions it is known as a solid figure or solid shape. It has length, breadth and height.

This cuboid is a solid figure.

➡ **three-dimensional**

solution noun

The solution to a problem is the answer or result.

eg I'm thinking of a number. If I halve it and add 3 I make 9. What is my number?

The solution to this problem is 12.

sort verb

To sort is to collect objects and numbers into different groups depending on chosen rules. The groups are known as sets.

eg Shapes can be sorted into sets of shapes with curved edges and straight edges.

➡ **Carroll diagram, set, Venn diagram**

south noun

South is one of the four main points of the compass, opposite to north.

eg

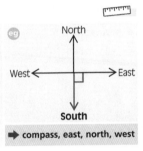

➡ **compass, east, north, west**

space noun

All objects take up space. The amount of space objects fill depends on their size or volume.

eg Capacity is the amount of space in a container.

➡ **capacity, volume**

speed noun

Speed tells you how fast something is moving. It is how far something moves in a certain amount of time.

eg The car travelled at a speed of 70 kilometres per hour (kph). In three hours it travelled 210 kilometres.

sphere noun

A sphere is a solid shape with a curved surface. All the points on the surface of a sphere are exactly the same distance from its centre.

eg

87

spherical adjective

A spherical object is an object shaped like a sphere.

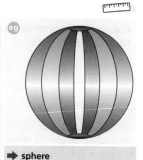

➡ sphere

spinner noun

A spinner is a top with numbers marked on it. A spinner is used for probability experiments.

eg The probability of landing on an odd number using this spinner is 1 in 3, or $\frac{1}{3}$.

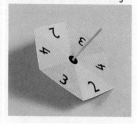

➡ probability

square

1 noun

A square is a flat shape with four straight and equal sides. The angles in its corners are all right angles.

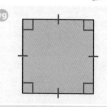

➡ quadrilateral

2 verb

To square a number is to multiply it by itself. You can show that a number is squared by writing a small number 2 just after and above the number, e.g. 5^2.

eg 5 squared is $5^2 = 5 \times 5 = 25$.

➡ square number

square-based pyramid ➡ pyramid

square centimetre (cm²) noun

A square centimetre is a unit of area – a square measuring 1cm × 1cm.

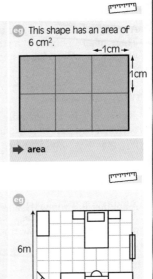

This shape has an area of 6 cm².

➡ area

square metre (m²) noun

A square metre is a unit of area – a square measuring 1m × 1m.

This room has an area of 48 m².

➡ area

square number noun

1 2 3 4

A square number is formed when a number is multiplied by itself. A square number can be arranged as a group of dots in the shape of a square. The number of dots is the same as the number itself. The first four square numbers are 1, 4, 9 and 16.

$1^2 = 1, 2^2 = 4, 3^2 = 9, 4^2 = 16$

➡ index, square

square root (√) noun

1 2 3 4

The square root of a number is the number that, when multiplied by itself, gives you the first number. 3 is the square root of 9. When 3 is squared (3 × 3) the answer is 9.

The square root of 49 is 7.
$\sqrt{49} = 7$

➡ square

statistics noun

Statistics are a collection of data or information which are displayed and analysed.

The statistics showed that the taller the person, the longer their arms.

stone noun

A stone is an imperial unit of weight. There are 14 pounds in a stone. 1 stone weighs just over 6 kilograms.

eg An average man weighs about 13 stone.

➡ pound

straight adjective

A straight line is the shortest distance between two points. It is a line that joins two points without bending.

eg A   B

This is a straight line between A and B.

subtraction (−) noun

Subtraction means taking one number away from another. The − sign shows that one number is being subtracted from another.

eg Subtract 15 from 20.
$$20 - 15 = 5$$

➡ difference, take away

sum noun

The sum of two or more numbers is the answer you get when you add them together.

eg The sum of the first three even numbers is 12.
$$2 + 4 + 6 = 12$$

➡ addition, total

surface noun

The surface of an object is its outside layer or boundary. It has no thickness. The surface area is the total area of the outside surface.

eg The surface of a cube consists of six square faces.

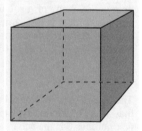

survey noun

Carrying out a survey involves collecting data so that it can be displayed and analysed.

eg The class carried out a traffic survey to analyse the road use outside their school.

symbol noun

A mark or sign standing for something is known as a symbol. There are many mathematical symbols, including numbers (1, 2, 3, 4 …), signs (+, −, ×, ÷) and notation (<, >. =, %).

eg The symbols for greater than and less than are > and <.

symmetrical adjective

A symmetrical shape is one that is balanced about a point, line or plane.

eg

symmetry noun

A shape has symmetry when two or more of its parts are matching shapes. If a figure keeps its shape when reflected or rotated it is said to have symmetry.

eg The letter A has line symmetry and the letter Z has rotational symmetry.

➡ line symmetry, rotational symmetry

table noun

A table is a list of numbers or information in rows and columns.

×	1	2	3
1	1	2	3
2	2	4	6
3	3	6	9

take away (−) verb

To take away is to remove items or numbers from an amount. The − sign shows that one number is being taken away from another.

eg 16 take away 7 equals 9.
16 − 7 = 9

➡ **difference, subtraction**

tally verb

To tally is to count by making marks. The most common method is to mark off sets of 5.

The word tally comes from the Latin word *talea*, meaning a stick.

car colour	tally	frequency
red	ⅢⅢ II	12
blue	Ⅲ II	7
white	III	3
total		22

tangram noun

A tangram is a Chinese puzzle in which a square is cut into five triangles, one square and one parallelogram. The shapes are then used to make different figures.

temperature noun

The temperature is a measure of how hot or how cold something is. Temperature is measured in degrees (°) as a number on a scale. The most common temperature scales are the Celsius (°C) scale and the Fahrenheit (°F) scale.

eg The temperature rose by 8°C today, reaching a maximum of 24°C.

➡ **Celsius, climate, Fahrenheit**

tenth (10th)

1 adjective
The tenth thing is the one after the ninth if they are put in order.

eg October is the tenth month in the year.

2 noun
A tenth ($\frac{1}{10}$) is a fraction. One-tenth is one out of ten parts.

eg A millimetre is a tenth of a centimetre.

tessellation noun

A tessellation is a pattern made by fitting plane shapes together without gaps.

Tessellation comes from the Latin word *tessella*, which was the name for a small piece of coloured stone used by the Romans to make mosaics.

tetrahedron noun

A tetrahedron is a solid shape with four triangular faces.
A regular tetrahedron has an equilateral triangle for each face.

➡ **pyramid**

thousandth

1 adjective
Thousandth (1000th) is the ordinal number of a thousand.

eg The thousandth person to visit the website was given a prize

2 adjective
A thousandth is the fraction $\frac{1}{1000}$.

eg A metre is a thousandth of a kilometre

three-dimensional (3D) adjective

A solid shape is three-dimensional because it has length, width and height.

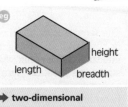

➡ **two-dimensional**

time noun

Time is an occasion or period measured in seconds, minutes and hours.

eg The actual time varies around the world. When it is midday in London it is 7.00 a.m. in New York.

➡ analogue clock, calendar, digital clock

times (×) verb

Times is a way of saying 'groups of' or 'lots of' in a multiplication fact.

eg 3 times 8 is 3 lots of 8 (8 + 8 + 8), which is 24.

➡ multiply

ton noun

A ton is a measure of mass or weight in the imperial system. A ton is 2240 pounds and is a little more than a tonne in the metric system.

eg A large car weighs about 1 ton.

➡ tonne

tonne noun

A tonne is a measure of mass or weight in the metric system. A tonne is 1000 kilograms (kg) and is a little less than a ton in the imperial system.

eg 10 large adults would weigh about 1 tonne.

➡ ton

torus noun

A torus is a solid ring shape with a hole in the middle.

eg

total noun

The total is the result when you add together a group of numbers.

eg The total of 6, 7 and 8 is 21.
6 + 7 + 8 = 21

➡ addition, sum

transformation noun

A transformation is a change made to the position and/or size of a shape.

eg Reflection, rotation and translation are all transformations.

➡ **reflection, rotation, translation**

translation noun

A translation is a movement of a shape in a straight line. Every point of a shape that is translated moves the same distance and direction.

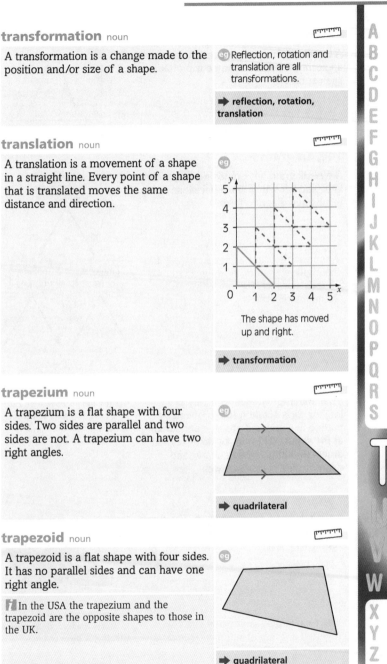

The shape has moved up and right.

➡ **transformation**

trapezium noun

A trapezium is a flat shape with four sides. Two sides are parallel and two sides are not. A trapezium can have two right angles.

➡ **quadrilateral**

trapezoid noun

A trapezoid is a flat shape with four sides. It has no parallel sides and can have one right angle.

In the USA the trapezium and the trapezoid are the opposite shapes to those in the UK.

➡ **quadrilateral**

A B C D E F G H I J K L M N O P Q R S T U V W X Y Z

travel graph noun

A travel graph is a line diagram showing a journey, in which distance is plotted against time.

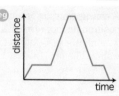

tree diagram noun

A tree diagram has branching, connecting lines and is used to show decisions or results in a diagram form.

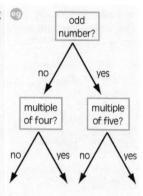

trial and improvement phrase

1234

Trial and improvement is a way of looking for a solution to a problem by putting in a guessed-at value and looking at the results. This can be done several times, each time getting nearer and nearer to the correct answer.

Trial and improvement can be used to work out the length of sides of a cube with a volume of 100 cm³.

triangle noun

A triangle is a 3-sided polygon. The three angles of a triangle always add up to 180°.

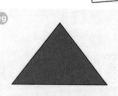

➡ equilateral triangle, isosceles triangle, right-angled triangle, scalene triangle

triangular number *noun*

1234

A triangular number can be arranged as a group of dots in the shape of a triangle. The number of dots is the same as the number itself. The first four triangular numbers are 1, 3, 6 and 10.

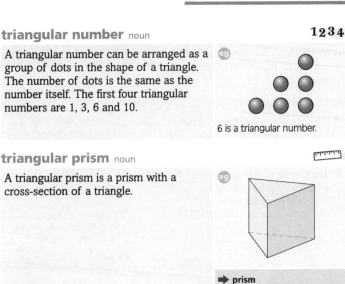

6 is a triangular number.

triangular prism *noun*

A triangular prism is a prism with a cross-section of a triangle.

➡ **prism**

trillion *noun*

1234

A trillion is one million million, written as 1 000 000 000 000.

ℹ In the UK, a trillion used to be 1 million million million, but this is no longer used.

The nearest star to Earth, apart from the sun, is Proxima Centauri, which is just under 40 trillion kilometres away!

➡ **billion, million**

triple

1 *verb*
To triple is to multiply by 3.

Triple 3 is 9.

2 *adjective*
The number that is three times another number is a triple.

9 is the triple of 3.

two-dimensional (2D) *adjective*

A flat shape is two-dimensional because it has length and width but no height (thickness).

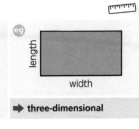

length

width

➡ **three-dimensional**

uncertain adjective

If something is uncertain you cannot say you are sure that it will happen. The event is doubtful or unsure.

On a probability scale the nearer to 0 an event is, the more uncertain it is.

➡ probability, probability scale

unfair adjective

When something is unfair it is biased.

A spinner labelled 1, 1, 1, 2, 2, 3, 3, 4 would give an unfair chance of spinning a 4.

➡ fair

unit

1 noun
A unit means one; a single thing or number.

1 unit of electricity cost 6.5 pence.

2 noun
A unit is the digit or position immediately to the left of the decimal point in a number.

In the number 38.6, the units value is 8.

3 noun
A unit of measurement is a standard amount of that measurement.

A metre is a unit of measurement equal to 100 cm.

unitary method noun

The unitary method is a method used in problems which involve calculating the value of one item and multiplying by the number of items required.

Sam pays £8.50 for 5 pens. How much will he pay for 3 pens? A single pen costs £1.70 (£8.50 ÷ 5) so 3 pens cost 3 × £1.70 which is £5.10.

unit fraction noun

A unit fraction has a numerator of 1 and any number as the denominator.

$\frac{1}{2}$, $\frac{1}{7}$, $\frac{1}{25}$ are all unit fractions.

➡ denominator, fraction, numerator, proper fraction

unlikely adjective

If the probability of an event is unlikely the chance of it happening is very small. The event is unlikely to happen, although it is possible.

It is unlikely that it will snow in London in August.

➡ probability, probability scale

V is the symbol which stands for 5 in the Roman number system.

eg VIII stands for the number 8.

➡ **Roman numerals**

Venn diagram *noun*

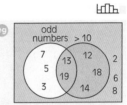

A Venn diagram is a way of showing how different things can be sorted into groups. The groups are known as sets.

eg

🔸 Venn diagrams are named after the mathematician John Venn (1834–1923).

odd numbers   > 10

7   13   12   2
5   19   18   6
3   14   8

➡ **Carroll diagram, set, sort**

vertex (plural: vertices) *noun*

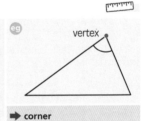

A vertex is a point where two or more lines meet to make an angle. It is one of the corners of a triangle, square or any polygon or solid shape.

eg vertex

➡ **corner**

vertical *adjective*

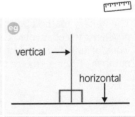

1 *noun*
Vertical means at right angles to the horizontal.

vertical ➡

2 *adjective*
A vertical line is at right angles to a horizontal line

horizontal

🔸 A builder uses a plumb bob, which is a heavy weight on a string, to check that a wall is vertical. The force of gravity pulls the weight towards the centre of the earth, which makes the string hang down vertically.

➡ **horizontal**

volume – vulgar fraction

A
B
C
D
E
F
G
H
I
J
K
L
M
N
O
P
Q
R
S
T
U
V
W
X
Y
Z

volume noun

The volume of an object is the amount of space it fills. It is measured in cubic centimetres (cm³) and cubic metres (m³). To find the volume you multiply the length by the breadth by the height. It is sometimes written as: l × b × h.

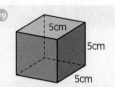

The volume of this cube
is 5cm × 5cm × 5cm = 125 cm³.

➡ capacity

vulgar fraction ➡ common fraction

A B C D E F G H I J K L M N O P Q R S T U V W X Y Z

week noun

A week is a period of seven days. A year has 52 weeks and one day (or two days in a leap year).

eg Monday, Tuesday, Wednesday, Thursday, Friday, Saturday and Sunday are the days of the week.

➡ year

weigh verb

You weigh something to find out how heavy it is.

eg The bag of sugar weighed 1 kg.

weight noun

Weight is the heaviness of an object or person. A force called gravity pulls objects down and gives them weight. We usually measure weight in kilograms (kg) which are really units for measuring mass.

eg My friend is the same weight as me.

➡ mass

west noun

West is one of the four main points of the compass, opposite to east and 90° anticlockwise of north.

eg

North
West ⟵ ⟶ East
South

➡ compass, east, north, south

whole number noun

1 2 3 4

Whole numbers is a loose term and can mean both natural numbers (1, 2, 3 etc.), or integers, so they can be positive or negative numbers. They have no parts that are fractions and they can include zero.

eg The whole numbers between 3 and 7 are 4, 5 and 6.

➡ integer, natural number

width noun

Width is another name for breadth. It is a measure of how wide something is – the distance across from one side to the other.

eg

45m

The width of this river is 45 metres.

➡ breadth, length

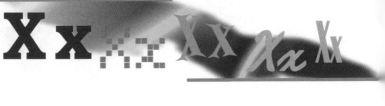

X

1 2 3 4

X is the symbol which stands for 10 in the Roman number system.

> XX stands for the number 20.

➡ **Roman numerals**

x-axis noun

The horizontal axis on a graph is the *x*-axis.

> *y*
>
> x-axis
>
> 0   *x*

➡ **axis, y-axis**

Yy

yard noun

A yard is a measure of length in the imperial system. There are three feet in one yard.

A yard was the distance from a man's nose to the tip of his outstretched arm. It had to be standardised because of different arm lengths.

eg 1 yard is approximately equal to 1 metre and is about the length of a long stride made by an adult.

➡ foot, inch, metre

y-axis noun

The vertical axis on a graph is the y-axis.

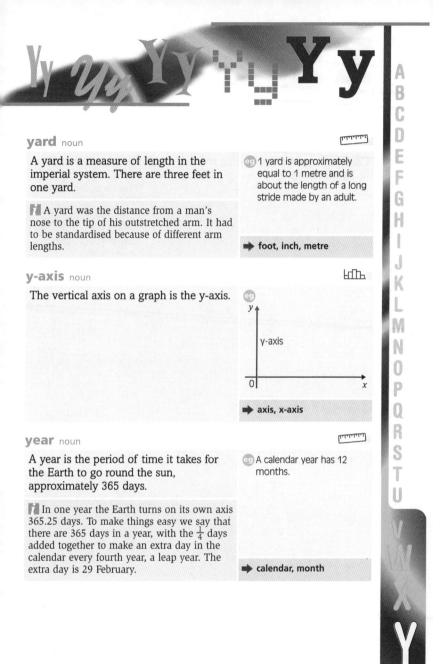

eg

➡ axis, x-axis

year noun

A year is the period of time it takes for the Earth to go round the sun, approximately 365 days.

In one year the Earth turns on its own axis 365.25 days. To make things easy we say that there are 365 days in a year, with the $\frac{1}{4}$ days added together to make an extra day in the calendar every fourth year, a leap year. The extra day is 29 February.

eg A calendar year has 12 months.

➡ calendar, month

zero (0) noun

Zero is the symbol for nothing or nought.
It is written as 0.

Three plus zero equals
three.

Three minus zero equals
three.

Three multiplied by zero
equals zero.

Three divided by zero
equals infinity.